FOREVER FREE
Elsa's Pride

JOY ADAMSON

FOREVER FREE

Elsa's Pride

An abridged edition for
young readers

COLLINS: LIONS

First published 1962 by William Collins Sons and Co Ltd
14 St James's Place, London SW1
First published in this abridged edition in Lions 1972
8th Impression 1976

Printed in Great Britain
by Richard Clay (The Chaucer Press) Ltd
Bungay, Suffolk

CONTENTS

To all who help in
the conservation of wild life

1 THE DEPORTATION ORDER

It was on Christmas Eve 1960 that we received a letter from the African District Council ordering us to remove Elsa and her cubs from the reserve. The reason given by the council was that since Elsa was used to our company she might become a danger to other people.

We were amazed: the local authorities themselves had helped us to choose the area for her release, and up to now had regarded her as a great asset to the reserve. It had been her home for two and a half years, and during that time she had never hurt anyone. But all we could do was to try to make this removal as little harmful to the lions as possible and find a satisfactory new home for them. We wrote to friends in Tanganyika, Uganda, Rhodesia and South Africa, inquiring what the chances were of finding a good territory for the family in their countries, but, before finally deciding to remove Elsa and her family from Kenya, George wished to carry out a reconnaissance along the eastern shores of Lake Rudolf in the north of Kenya.

I was distressed by this plan. The country there is very grim, and I feared that game around the lake might be so scarce that Elsa and the cubs would become dependent upon us for their food supply. Besides this, the area is so remote that in case of an emergency we should be very lucky if we were able to get any help. On the other hand, this very remoteness was perhaps an asset.

So, while we waited for replies to our letters, we made provisional plans for their removal to Lake Rudolf. We estimated that the journey would take two or three days and nights: we knew that the tracks would be very rough and that we should need to tow the cars through sandy river-beds, stretches of desert and over rocky escarpments.

To make the experiment we would first build a ramp and then place a five-ton lorry against it so that its floor was level with the

7

top of the ramp; in the lorry we would place the lions' dinner. Once the cubs had got used to their new feeding place we could build a strong wire enclosure over the lorry and make a trap door to it, which we would close when the cubs were feeding, thus converting the lorry into a travelling crate.

We dug the ramp at the salt-lick near the studio. My heart was heavy as I watched the cubs; they were excited by the unusual activities taking place on their playground, sniffed the freshly dug soil curiously, found it great fun to roll on the earth, and seemed to think that all this work was being done to amuse them.

On 28th December George left camp and after a few days at Isiolo started off on the recce to Lake Rudolf. That afternoon I met the family near the river, and after the usual friendly greetings from Elsa and Jespah, we went together to the water's edge. The cubs plunged in at once, ducking and chasing each other; Elsa and I watched them from the bank. While they were in the river she guarded them in a dignified manner, but when they emerged dripping wet joined in their games and helped them to look for a new playground. A nearby tree provided what was needed, the cubs struggled up its trunk but were soon overtaken by their mother, who in a few swift movements leapt high above them. She went higher and higher, the slender upper branches bending alarmingly beneath her weight until finally she reached the crown of the tree. When she found that the boughs were no longer strong enough to support her, she turned with great difficulty and, cautiously testing each branch, began her descent. She managed to make her way down but her landing was by no means dignified, then, as though to suggest that the tumble was a joke, she at once began to jump around the cubs. They chased her, and all the way home played games of hide-and-seek or ambushes, in which I was often the victim.

Next day the family appeared on the far bank of the river opposite the studio. I had seen a six-foot crocodile slither into the river at their approach and was therefore not surprised when the cubs paced nervously up and down the rocky platform by the river's edge, obviously frightened to jump into the deep pool beneath.

Elsa licked each in turn, then they all plunged in together and swam safely across in close formation. When the cubs relaxed and began to chase each other so as to get dry, Elsa joined in. She took Jespah's tail in her mouth and walked round in circles with him, obviously enjoying the clowning as much as he did.

Eventually Jespah sat down close to me, turning his back to me. This he did when he wanted to be petted; he seemed to realise that I was always a little afraid of being accidentally scratched by him because, unlike his mother, he had not learnt to retract his claws when playing with human beings.

On the first of January I felt very apprehensive. What would the New Year bring? On the 2nd of January, Ken Smith and Peter Saw, both game wardens from adjoining districts, arrived in a lorry. They had come with the consent of the Game Department to offer their help in moving Elsa and the cubs.

Ken had been on the lion hunt which brought Elsa into our life and had visited her twice since then, but he had never seen the cubs, so we all went off to look for the family. We found them in the studio lugga ('lugga' is Somali for dry river bed), but at the sight of two strangers the cubs bolted. Elsa greeted Ken as an old friend, but paid no attention to Peter. When our guests came close to Elsa, Jespah peeped anxiously through the foliage, obviously prepared to defend his mother if the need arose. Eventually he came into the open, though he kept at a safe distance.

The cubs were becoming increasingly shy of strangers. Jespah had overcome his suspicion of George and myself, but he didn't trust anyone else.

He showed his confidence in me on the following day, when he allowed me to rid him of a couple of maggots. Jespah kept absolutely still while I attended to his maggots, then he licked his wounds and placed himself in his safety position, inviting me to pat him. For the first time, he even allowed me to touch his silky nostrils; perhaps he wanted to show me that he was grateful for my help.

That evening he came alone into the tent, squatted in his safety position, and kept quite still until I stroked him. His demands for affection posed a serious problem: I hated to disappoint him but,

9

on the other hand, apart from my fear of his claws, we wanted the cubs to develop into wild lions, and Jespah's friendliness was already jeopardising his future. Gopa and Little Elsa were different; their reactions were always those of wild animals.

The next day our Thames lorry arrived. We hoped to teach Elsa and the cubs to feed in it, so we gave it a thorough wash and then parked it at the ramp, but it smelt of petrol, oil and Africans, and nothing would persuade the cubs to go near it. Even Elsa would not follow me into it, although I tried every trick I could think of to persuade her, in the belief that her example would encourage the cubs. There was nothing to be done except to wait until the lions had overcome their suspicion of the lorry.

It was six days since we had placed the lorry by the ramp and, so far as I could judge from the spoor, no lion had been near it. I went into the open truck and called to Elsa; after some hesitation she followed me, but placed herself broadside on to the entrance, thus preventing me from getting out or Jespah, who was following her, from coming in. After a time she went back to the tents and hopped on to the roof of the Land-Rover. The cubs began to eat and I went over to their mother and started to play with her; as I did so, I noticed that she had been attacked by maggots and that two of the swellings had gone septic. I wanted to deal with them, but each time I touched her she withdrew, and when on the following day I again tried to help her she seemed to be even more sensitive. But I presumed that she would lick her wounds clean, as she had often done before when she had been plagued by the maggots.

George had now been away for two weeks on the recce to Lake Rudolf. He had been joined by Ken Smith and the game warden for the area. I expected them back any day but almost dreaded to hear the noise of the car, for I feared it might mean the end of Elsa's happy life. What would await her in her new home? How many lionesses might she have to conquer before her territory was safe for the cubs? She loved her home and here she had at least established her rights. She and her children would need to forget this ideal environment and all that was familiar to them before they could begin to be happy in another place.

One night I heard the family around the camp, and it was not until after breakfast that they scampered towards the doam-palm logs beyond the salt-lick, where Elsa stood contemplating the lorry. Very soon she stepped cautiously on to the roof of the cabin and sat down. For ten days I had been waiting for her to do just this, but now I felt sad to see her sitting so trustingly on the lorry which was to take her away from her home.

I joined her and tried, without success, to deal with her maggots. She was licking them, and I saw that she had seven swellings, but, as at times she had had as many as fifteen, I was not unduly alarmed.

All that afternoon Elsa rested on the cabin roof, from which she watched her cubs and me. When I went for a short walk she did not follow me. After it got dark she came and lay in the grass in front of my tent, but made no attempt to hop on to the roof of the Land-Rover as she usually did. I walked up to her, but was charged by Gopa and Jespah who had been resting nearby in the tall grass.

Early next morning I heard Elsa calling to the cubs in her soft moan, 'Mhm, mhm, mhm'; it was a most comforting sound and always had a very soothing effect on me.

Soon they all disappeared in the direction of the studio lugga; in the afternoon I took a sketch-book and went there. Elsa welcomed me gently and affectionately, and even Gopa showed a sign of friendliness by tilting his head towards me. We spent a lovely afternoon, the cubs playing as I drew. I would have been completely happy but for the apprehension which nagged at me when I thought of the cruel move from which only a miracle could save us. I hoped that Elsa didn't sense my wretchedness and anxiety; she was ill enough as it was with her maggot sores.

When she thought it was time for us to go home she gave us her usual signal by licking each of us in turn. I wondered how long she would be able to maintain the friendly relations which existed between the five of us. For how much longer would I be accepted as a member of the pride? If we succeeded in enabling the cubs to live natural wild lives this would in any case bring the relationship to an end. Our intimate life with the lions had only lasted as long

11

as it had because the threat of attack by poachers had compelled us to stay with the family to protect them. On the other hand, if the lions were removed to Lake Rudolf the possibility of their taking up a full wild life would be delayed or even become impracticable. This might be inevitable, but for them to be denied their natural life simply so that I should retain my position as part of the pride was too high a price to pay for my privilege.

Elsa was constantly licking her wounds; I hoped this would help to heal them quickly. That night she again stayed in the grass outside my tent and refused to eat. As I was watching her, Gopa came up to me and wished to make friends. This was unusual, and I wanted to respond, but like Jespah, he had not learned to retract his claws when playing with human beings, so reluctantly I had to disappoint him. I squatted near him, looking him in the face, calling him by his name and hoping that he would understand that even if I would not play with him, all the same I loved him. Jespah brought this awkward situation to an end by bouncing on his brother. The manes of the two lions had grown a lot lately; Gopa's was much darker and nearly twice the length of his brother's; his growl was deep and sometimes threatening. In every way he was a powerful young lion.

Next afternoon I again found the family in the studio lugga. Elsa lay quite still and allowed me to pat her, but when I touched her back, or my hand came near one of her sores, she growled and made it very plain that she did not want me to interfere. Her nose was wet and cold; a sure sign that she was ill. Two of the wounds were festering and pus was oozing out of them. I hoped that this meant that they would drain.

Several days later I went to the Whuffing Rock with Nuru; Elsa at once came out of the bush below the rock, followed by Jespah. She greeted us affectionately, but I noticed that she was breathing heavily and that every movement seemed to require an effort. Jespah acted like a bodyguard and made it difficult for me to stroke her. I sat close to her till Gopa and Little Elsa joined us and then we all started for home. Elsa was very impatient with the cubs and evidently extremely sensitive to being touched. If one of her children brushed against her, she flattened her ears and

12

growled. She did not, however, object to my walking beside her and flicking off the tsetse flies, but got really angry when one of the cubs tried to prod her. I had never before seen her react like this. She sat down repeatedly during the short distance through the bush to the car track, but after we reached the track the going was easier. When we got to the camp she went straight up to the Land-Rover and lay down on the roof very carefully to avoid putting pressure on her sores. She stayed in this position all through the evening. I brought her some marrow, a thing she loved, but she only looked at it and turned away, and when I tried to stroke her paws she moved them out of my reach.

Soon it would be four weeks since we had received the deportation order and it was already three since George had gone on his recce to Lake Rudolf. Before he left, we had planned to start the move on the 20th of January; today was the 19th; never once had the cubs entered the Thames lorry; the Bedford had not arrived, Elsa was ill, we had not yet found a new home for the cubs or a way of moving them. Plainly, we were going to be far behind our schedule.

2 ELSA'S DEATH

That evening George arrived. He and Ken Smith had carried out a thorough and gruelling reconnaissance around the area of Lake Rudolf to find a suitable home for Elsa and her cubs. Their opinion was that Moite offered the only hope, and this only if George could find or make a passable route to it and get permission to rent some land there. There was enough game for the needs of Elsa and the cubs, and a few lions in the area for company and mating. The area was very remote and, as we had supposed, unlikely to become the scene of political complications.

These were the assets; there were also many drawbacks.

To say that the country round Moite is grim is an understatement. It consists solely of sand and lava, is swept by storms, and the sun blazes fiercely down upon it; in fact, it is only made tolerable by the waters of the lake.

Before returning to Isiolo, George discussed with the District Commissioner of Marsabit the possibility of renting some land round Moite, and asked for his co-operation in building a 600-mile road and clearing the ground for an airstrip. The District Commissioner gave his consent. We, of course, were to provide the necessary cash. Since the sum involved was considerable, George said he would wait to take a decision until he had discussed the matter with me.

The prospect of settling the lions near Lake Rudolf seemed very unsatisfactory to me. Even if, by renting land at Moite, we could ensure that they would not be tempted to injure the tribesmen's stock in the area, how could we prevent Elsa and the cubs from leaving this sanctuary? The local lions might object to their presence and what would happen if they were driven into the waterless hinterland? I also feared that once we had built a road it would inevitably be used and, if so, would it not end by evoking the same fears which were the reason for exiling Elsa and the

14

cubs from their present home? For all these reasons I was not at all happy about the prospect of the move to Moite and was much relieved that we found letters from Rhodesia, Bechuanaland and South Africa in reply to our inquiries, all offering alternative possibilities.

However, since we had no idea whether the ecological conditions in these areas would be suitable for our lions, George suggested that I should go at once to Nairobi and ask the advice of Major Ian Grimwood, our Chief Game Warden, who knew these localities well. As there was so little time left, I agreed to go, provided that Elsa was well enough for me to leave her.

That evening we did not see the lions, but we heard them on the far side of the river, so hoped that they were all right. Early next morning we waded to the opposite bank and found the family a few yards from the water. Elsa broke through the dense undergrowth and rubbed herself affectionately against me. I scratched her on the head and behind the ears. Her coat was like velvet and her body hard and strong.

George did not think she looked any worse than she had on earlier occasions when she had been infested with maggots, and this relieved my anxiety. However, as she had not eaten for two days, before I left, we placed meat on the river bank; while we did this Elsa watched us from the far side. As she made no attempt to come over and collect it, George floated it across; he had to put it right in front of her before she rose and, without eating anything herself, dragged it up the steep slope and into the thicket where the cubs were.

With this last picture of Elsa helping her children, I reluctantly left the camp.

I arrived in Nairobi and went to keep my first appointment which was with the Chief Game Warden, but before we had started our discussion he handed me a telegram from George:

Elsa worse. Has high fever. Suggest bring aureomycin.

The message had been telephoned through from Isiolo by Ken, who had asked Major Grimwood to tell me that he had already sent the drug to George. I was terribly worried, but I knew I must stay one night in Nairobi.

Major Grimwood told me that in the homes offered in Rhodesia and Bechuanaland the ecological conditions would not suit Elsa or the cubs, therefore he advised us to move the lions to Lake Rudolf. So I telegraphed to the District Commissioner at Marsabit asking him to start on the work which George had discussed with him.

Next morning when I came downstairs I found Ken waiting for me. He had just arrived from Isiolo with a message from George that Elsa was now desperately ill. George had sent an SOS at midnight, asking for me to return and for a vet to come at once. Ken had got in touch with John MacDonald, the vet at Isiolo, who had left immediately, then Ken had driven the one hundred and eighty miles to Nairobi to give me George's message.

I chartered a plane and soon Ken and I were on our way. We arrived at the camp about tea-time. I rushed to the studio. George was sitting there alone, and looked at me without saying anything. His expression told more than I could bear. When I had recovered from the shock he took me to Elsa's grave.

It was under a tree close to the tents, overlooking the river and the sand-bank where Elsa had introduced me to her children. This was the tree on whose rough bark the cubs had learned to sharpen their claws; under the shade of which the family had so often played.

George told me all that had happened while I was away. This is what he said:

'The night after you left, I found Elsa lying under a bush a little farther up the river. She got up and greeted me and Makedde. The cubs came along and played around their mother.

'I then went back to camp; that night no lions appeared. Before breakfast I went to look for Elsa; she was lying alone near the place where I had left her the night before. She replied to my calls, but did not get up to greet me. Her breathing was laboured and she seemed to be in pain. I returned to camp to telegram you.

'Then I went back to Elsa with water and a plate of meat and brains into which I had mixed sulphathiazole. She drank a little water but, even in spite of her liking for brains, did not eat anything. I then put some sulphathiazole into the water, but she refused it. I felt very much alarmed, for she was steadily growing weaker.

'To leave her alone for the night was unthinkable, for in her weak state she might have been attacked by hyenas, buffalo or by a lioness. I therefore decided to spend the night with her, and got the boys to bring my bed over from the camp, also the remains of the goat and a pressure lamp. Elsa seemed to be a little better. Twice she came up to my bed and rubbed her head affectionately against me.

'At dawn Elsa seemed fairly comfortable, so I went back to camp for breakfast and then did some typing.

'About ten o'clock I began to feel anxious and went to look for Elsa. I could not find her; there was no answer to my calls and no sign of the cubs. For two hours I searched up and down the river and at last I found her lying half in the water by a little island near the camp. She looked desperately ill, her breathing was very fast and she was extremely weak. I tried to give her water in my cupped hands but she could not swallow.

'I stayed with her for an hour. Then Elsa suddenly made an immense effort and went up the steep bank on to the island, where she collapsed. I called Nuru and got him to cut a path to a place from which it was easy to cross the river. Then, I left Nuru in charge, and went back to camp and improvised a stretcher out of my camp-bed and tent poles. When this was ready I carried it back to the island and laid it beside Elsa, hoping that, since she always liked lying on a bed, she might roll on to it. If she did this, I meant, with the help of the men, to carry her across the river to my tent. But Elsa did not attempt to get on to the bed. About three o'clock she suddenly rose to her feet and staggered to the river. With my help she waded across it to the bank below the kitchen. She was completely exhausted by the effort and lay for a long time on the bank. At least now she was on our side of the river and close to the camp.

'For the next two hours Elsa lay on the sand-bank with Jespah close to her. Twice she got up and went to the water's edge to drink, but she could not swallow. It was a pathetic sight. I tried pouring water from my cupped hands into her mouth but it just dribbled out again. When it got dark she walked up the narrow path and lay down at the place where my tent used to stand before I moved it up to the ramp.

'I tried to give her a little milk and whisky by squirting it into her mouth with a syringe; she managed to swallow some of it. Then I covered her with a blanket and hoped she would not move. I was in despair, feeling sure that she would not last out the night, anxious to send a message to you and worried because the truck was very much overdue. I realised that the only hope of saving her was to get a vet as quickly as possible; on the other hand, I did not want to leave her in case she wandered off in the darkness, in which case it might have been impossible to find her.

'In the end, I decided to risk leaving her for an hour and a half, the time it would take me to go to and from a bad ford where I thought the truck might be stuck. Less than two miles from camp I met the truck which had got stuck both going to and returning from Isiolo. The driver had brought the drug for Elsa. I wrote a letter to Ken, telling him that Elsa was in desperate need of a vet and asked him to get in touch with you. Then I sent the driver straight back to Isiolo in my Land-Rover.

'Fortunately Elsa had not moved. It was impossible to get her to swallow the drug. She had become very restless, would get up, move a few paces and then lie down again. All my attempts to make her drink failed.

'At about eleven at night she moved into my tent near the studio and lay there for an hour. Then she got up, walked slowly down to the river, waded in and stood there for several minutes making attempts to drink but unable to swallow. Eventually, she returned to my tent and again lay down in it.

'The cubs came to the tent and Jespah nuzzled his mother, but she did not respond.

'At about a quarter to two in the morning, Elsa left the tent and went back to the studio and into the water. I tried to stop her, but she went resolutely on till she reached the sand-bank under the trees where she had so often played with the cubs. Here she lay on the sodden mud-bank, evidently in great distress, alternately sitting up and lying down, her breathing more laboured than ever.

18

'I tried to move her back to the dry sand of the studio, but she seemed beyond making any effort. It was a terrible and harrowing sight. It even crossed my mind that I ought to put her out of her misery, but I believed that there was still a chance that you might arrive with a vet in time to help her.

'At about 4.30 I called all the men in camp and with their help put Elsa on the stretcher and with much difficulty carried her back to my tent. She settled down and I lay beside her, completely exhausted.

'As dawn was breaking, she suddenly got up, walked to the front of the tent and collapsed. I held her head in my lap. A few minutes later she sat up, gave a most heart-rending terrible cry and fell over.

'Elsa was dead.'

Half an hour after Elsa died, John MacDonald, the Senior Veterinary Officer from Isiolo, arrived. Although George hated the idea, he agreed in the interests of medicine and of the cubs themselves, that a post-mortem should be carried out to establish the cause of death.

When this was over, Elsa was buried under the acacia tree where she had often rested; at George's command the game scouts fired three volleys over the grave. The reports echoed back from Elsa's rock. It was 24th January, 1961.

3 HAVE THE CUBS FOUND A PRIDE?

Now we were the guardians of Elsa's children.

It was a week since Elsa had died. We had expected her children to become dependent upon us, but in fact they had avoided us as far as hunger permitted. We would have to regain the trust of the cubs, who would need our help for at least another ten months. It was exactly a year since Elsa had brought them over the river to introduce them to us.

We had now received the result of Elsa's post-mortem. She had died of an infection by a tick-borne parasite called babesia, which destroys the red blood corpuscles. The four per cent infection which they found had proved fatal because of the weak condition to which she had been reduced by the bites of the mango flies. It was the first time that such an infection had been found in a lion.

I went to Isiolo to meet Major Grimwood and discuss the cubs' future with him. If it were necessary to move them we hoped that he would help us find a home for them in an East African game reserve. Major Grimwood proved most sympathetic, and promised to contact the authorities of the National Parks of Kenya and Tanganyika.

I brought an old crate back to camp with me. Now I hoped to induce the cubs to feed inside it. This was our plan: the cubs must get accustomed to feeding in the large communal crate, placed on the ground. Then, one day, when all three were inside, we would close the door and, disguising the tranquilliser in marrow, we would administer a dose in each of their three pie-dishes. We would push the dishes through a second door, small enough to prevent the cubs from escaping through it. We then intended to transfer them to three separate crates, specially designed to fit the back of a five-ton lorry.

I arrived about midnight and found all the cubs guarding their meat close to the tents. They did not mind the glare of the headlights, even when I turned them in their direction. We had noticed that though they were so nervous during the day, they showed little apprehension when it was dark. George had to return next morning to Isiolo, so I once more found myself in charge of the camp.

On the evening of the 10th of February, I was very happy to see the cubs chasing each other round the tents after their evening meal, for they had been distressingly subdued since their mother's death, and up to now had kept quiet after eating, just sitting still and watching.

Next evening I placed the crate in position and secured the meat near to it. When the cubs arrived at their usual time, Jespah after a few suspicious sniffs went into the crate. Then he came out and settled down near the meat with Gopa and Little Elsa. I talked to them in a low voice, hoping they would gradually learn to associate food with my presence. I now prepared three pie-dishes every day, filling each dish with a mixture of cod-liver oil, brain and marrow, hoping in this way to train the cubs to eat separately, so that when the time came to give them tranquillisers they would each get their ration of the drug, concealed in the titbits, and avoid the risk of any of them getting an overdose.

During the next three days, the lions kept to their routine – spending the days across the river, at the place where they had last been with their mother, and coming into camp after dark for their dinner. I did not interfere with their routine in any way, hoping that this would reassure them and make them trust me.

George's return from his trip to Isiolo coincided with Jespah's first meal inside the crate. Gopa and Little Elsa watched him but showed no desire to emulate him. However, after we had gone to bed they plucked up courage and both ventured into the crate to get their dinner. This was a great relief to us. Now that we knew that they were able to overcome their fear of this strange object, we felt that we must at once order the kind of crates in which they could be moved.

We decided to have three sides of the crates made of iron bars, so that during the journey the cubs would be able to see each other and, without being able to do any harm, could give each other moral support. There was, of course, a greater risk that they might get chafed against the bars, but we felt that this physical damage would heal more easily than a mind which had been injured by terror. The fourth side of the crates was to consist of a wooden trap door.

Having made up our minds about this, I set off to Nanyuki, two hundred and twenty miles away, to order the three travelling crates.

Very late on the night of my arrival back in camp Jespah appeared for a brief moment: evidently he had come as a scout to make sure that all was safe, for soon he returned with Gopa and Little Elsa. He took the cod-liver oil and let me pat him on the head, muzzle and ears, standing quite still as I did so. After the lights were out George saw Little Elsa join her two brothers in the crate which, with the three cubs and the 'kill' inside it was rather crowded.

More than twenty-four hours passed before I saw the cubs again; then in the early hours of the morning I heard their father's call, first from close by, and finally from near the Big Rock; and soon afterwards I heard the cubs lapping water out of the steel helmet which was still their favourite drinking bowl. I climbed out of the car to open the crate and give them access to their dinner, but they paid no attention to me and walked off determinedly towards the Big Rock, obviously more interested in joining their father than in having a meal. Was he, I wondered, perhaps helping to provide food for them? During the rest of the night I heard repeated whuffings from the rock, and next morning found the spoor of all the lions leading to it. To my disappointment, by next evening their father had deserted the cubs again; I heard him roaming round, and they came into camp very hungry. In spite of this they waited patiently for me to open the crate and rushed at the meat after I had got inside my 'sleeper'. They finished every scrap I had prepared for them before crossing the river at dawn.

On the 27th of February we found the cubs on the top of the Whuffing Rock. Jespah came when we called to him, sat close to me and tilted his head, but kept his eyes fixed on Gopa and his sister. After a time Little Elsa came a little nearer to us, but Gopa kept aloof and behaved as though we did not exist. It was a lovely

22

afternoon, peaceful and timeless; everything around us held memories of Elsa, and how like her Jespah was, with his intelligent expression and friendly, responsible nature.

As soon as we had come down from the rock Gopa and Little Elsa joined Jespah, and all stood silhouetted against the sunset. They seemed to be watching us intently. The cubs remained standing on the top of the rock until finally we were unable to make them out in the fading light.

During the next few nights the cubs stayed away from camp. George continued to search for the cubs and wrote me this note as I was away.

2nd March. During my afternoon search, found the tracks of three poachers or honey hunters crossing my morning spoor. It seems almost certain that the cubs have joined up with one or more lions down river, a long way below the cataract. I do not expect them back tonight. This is obviously their great adventure. Perhaps by now they are part of a new pride with their father and a stepmother.

I don't think you need worry unduly about them. They know the country well and are capable of finding their way back to camp if they want to; but for the moment I expect they are far too excited to think of the good meal waiting for them in camp – that will come later.

3rd March. The cubs did not turn up during the night. Set off about 7 a.m. this morning down river on the far bank. I crossed over and saw all three cubs – apparently they had just arrived from down river. Jespah came up and sat close to us while the others hid in the bush. We started back towards camp and after going a few hundred yards, stopped and waited for the cubs. Jespah appeared. But as it was the heat of the day I thought the cubs would lie up in the thick undergrowth. I returned to camp.

The cubs appeared about 7.30 p.m. not at all hungry, and up to now – 9.30 p.m. – have scarcely eaten anything, though Jespah promptly came up demanding his brain and cod-liver oil and took them out of my hand. They stayed all night, left about 5 a.m. and have gone towards Whuffing Rock.

George had to leave for Isiolo on the 5th of March, the day I arrived back in camp. That night no cubs appeared and I did not know whether to be pleased or worried. If they had joined up with a pride and were being taught to hunt by a lioness, then they would go wild before the question of deporting them arose; and this would probably be the best thing that could happen to them. On the other hand, they might have been driven away from the camp by the wild lions and be in desperate need of help.

The uncertainty of not knowing what had happened to them was distressing. The next day again passed without the cubs putting in an appearance.

Nuru and Makedde spent the next day tracking, but found no fresh spoor. In the early hours of the following morning I heard several lions roar, accompanied by the shrieking of baboons upstream. It seemed as though the lions were rapidly approaching the camp, for the roars came from nearby and grew louder, until suddenly they stopped. I lay awake listening, but heard no lion calls until two hours later, when they came from far upstream. When I got up I was surprised to see the pug marks of a lion and a lioness right up beside the car I had been sleeping in. The men went off tracking, but saw no sign of the cubs.

Another day and night passed without news of the cubs before George returned. He made a fruitless search that afternoon. Next morning he and Nuru set out again. Beyond the cataract they found the cubs' spoor coming from the elephant lugga down to the water and back again. The pug marks turned into running tracks, which suggested that the cubs had heard or scented their pursuers.

All night I listened to a single lion roaring on the Big Rock. Early in the morning George went spoor tracking. He told me that he and Nuru had put up at least four lions below the cataract. As they were bolting, Nuru caught sight of a cub which he felt convinced was Jespah. The running spoor seemed to confirm this, as among them were the pug marks of three cubs. George waited, hoping that at least Jespah might return; then, after an hour, he followed the tracks and found a place where a cub had evidently been lying down only a few minutes earlier. Feeling sure now that the cubs had been adopted by a pride, George did not pursue them for fear of upsetting the foster-parents.

Most nights now we heard two lions roaring round the camp: George thought he recognised their calls as those of the Fierce Lioness, who had once attacked Elsa, and her mate. We believed that this pair was not part of the pride which had apparently adopted Elsa's cubs.

During the next few days, George found the spoor of at least five lions, of which three were cubs. It seemed that this pride always stayed between the cataracts and the elephant lugga. This would, we thought, be an ideal home for our cubs; there was plenty of game and comparative safety from poachers. We could not be certain but we began to believe that the cubs had themselves solved the problem of their future, for we had not seen them for twelve days.

4 CRISIS

On the 16th of March George and Nuru left early for their daily search. I was alone in camp when two Game Scouts and an informer arrived to report that during the night of the 13th/14th three lions had attacked the bomas of tribesmen on the Tana River and mauled four cows. The Africans believed that the raiders were Elsa's cubs and they begged George to come and dispose of them.

I immediately sent the men to contact George, which they eventually did by firing shots. They all returned to camp and after lunch set off for the scene of the raids.

In all there were eight bomas within a short distance of each other, protected by a shoulder-high thorn fence some six foot wide. The country surrounding the bomas was dense bush, which meant that a lion could approach the huts without being seen. The bomas were close to the River Tana, where the tribesmen watered their stock.

On the following night they had mauled two more cows before being chased away, and on the third night they had killed two cows at a different boma from the one they had previously raided, and had eaten one of them within three hundred yards of the hut.

George saw the spoor of a lioness; she had entered an almost impenetrable thorn enclosure and then forced her way out of it. He then tried to examine other lion spoor, but had difficulty in doing so as most of the pug marks were obliterated by cattle tracks. However, he managed to trace the lions back to the place on the river bank where they had drunk and came upon new pug marks made by three lions.

With two scouts and a guide he took up this spoor. About an hour later they were casting about in a dry watercourse covered with thick vegetation when suddenly about ten feet away he saw a lioness lying asleep, partly concealed by the trunk of a tree.

He watched her for several minutes; she looked like a mature lioness. A scout who was a few paces behind signalled to George and tapped his rifle. In a whisper the scout urged George to shoot, saying that it was a full-grown lioness. It would have been very easy to put a bullet into her brain. But something made George hesitate. Suddenly, the lioness sat up and looked straight into his eyes. She wrinkled her face into a snarl, and, giving a low growl, dashed off. Simultaneously, he heard two other lions break away. He felt convinced that these were not our cubs, but was glad all the same that he had not fired, for how could he be quite certain? He called the cubs by name, but there was no response. Facts which helped to strengthen his belief that these raids were not the work of our cubs were the cunning manner in which the lions had attacked the village and forced their way through the particularly strong thorn fence, and also the apparent ease with which the two fully grown cows had been killed. All this suggested the work of experienced lions.

George told the tribesmen to report any further raids immediately, and then returned to camp. Discussing the circumstances of the raids together, we came to the conclusion that it was so improbable that Elsa's cubs would be involved that we decided to take up the search again in our own area.

The next morning George headed off to a drinking place higher upstream. Near the mouth of the elephant lugga, he saw two cubs resting on an island in the river; but they bolted before he could focus his field-glasses. Simultaneously, he heard more lions breaking away. Following their spoor, he came upon the carcase of a young buffalo which must have been killed the night before. Five lions had feasted on it. George felt sure these must have been Elsa's cubs and their foster-parents. He called to Jespah, and went on doing so for a long time, and thought he heard a faint moan from the far side of the river, but no cub came in sight, so he returned to camp.

George returned from his search and had to go at once to Isiolo to attend to some court cases.

All through the next night heavy rains fell and by the morning the river was only just fordable. Nevertheless, an informer managed to get across. He brought a message from the headman of the Tana settlement stating that their stock had again been raided by lions.

I sent Ibrahim to Isiolo to tell George the news. He came back with the message that George would go to the Tana village as soon as the court cases were over. Meanwhile the corporal in charge of the game scout post up river was to go there at once and take the thunder-flashes which George had sent back by Ibrahim. These were to frighten off the lions until he got there himself. George also sent instructions that no lions were to be shot before his arrival.

I passed on these instructions to the corporal, and he set off with the thunder-flashes, but, stopping on his way he heard that the local chief at the Tana had not only told his people to kill the lions but had also sent more game scouts of the neighbouring district to deal with the situation. The corporal instead of then making his way as rapidly as possible to the Tana to convey George's orders, returned to camp to give me the account he had just heard. I was horrified at the loss of time, and sent him packing off to the Tana, praying that he might arrive before one or more of the cubs had been killed – if, indeed, the raiders were Elsa's children.

George returned from Isiolo and the next morning set off in his Land-Rover for the scene of the last Tana raid. It had been raining heavily, so he was obliged to take a circuitous route. I remained in camp to keep a lookout in case the cubs were still in our area.

On the following day, as it was getting dark, I heard a lion roaring from the Big Rock; it was answered from farther away by another lion. Next I heard the roars advancing towards the kitchen lugga. Hoping that our cubs might be in the company of this lion, I told the men to prepare a meal for them. While this was being done, I was startled by a chorus of roars. It sounded as if there were lions on every side of the camp. Hurriedly we secured the meat inside my truck, and I advised the men to barricade themselves as best they could inside their thorn enclosure; I did the same myself and went to bed. There was no question of going to sleep for during the entire night we were kept awake by growls and

28

whuffings which only at dawn ebbed away in the direction of the Big Rock.

In the morning I went to Elsa's grave, and while I was there noticed some movement on the Big Rock. Looking through my field-glasses, I saw two lions basking on top of the rock. I walked towards them and soon distinguished three adult lions and three cubs exactly the size of Elsa's children. They were on top of the ridge, outlined against the sky. I watched them for several minutes; they were resting quietly together, one lioness licking the cubs who were rolling on their backs and playing. When I was within about four hundred yards of them, the lions became alarmed and one after the other disappeared into the gap where Elsa had started her labour. Only one cub remained behind. It crouched with its head on its forepaws, watching me. This behaviour made me think that it was probably Jespah. Unfortunately, as it sat right against the morning sun, I could only see its silhouette and could not pick out any details to confirm its identity. When I tried to come nearer, the cub sneaked away.

The idyllic family scene I had witnessed made me feel happier than I had felt since Elsa's death. Though I could not be quite sure that these were her children with their foster-parents, it seemed too great a coincidence that a pair of lions with three cubs exactly the same age as hers should suddenly have appeared near the camp.

After telling the men my exciting news, we put a carcase into the Land-Rover and I drove with Ibrahim near to the Big Rock, and placed the meat where I thought the lions would find it easily. Then we camouflaged the car with branches and waited inside to see what would happen. I hoped to take some photographs when the cubs reappeared, and so identify them.

We waited till 11 o'clock; by then the sun was getting hot, the wind changed and was blowing in the wrong direction, and to my disappointment, no vultures had appeared to guide the lions to the kill.

When I returned to camp, I found a letter from George. This is what he wrote:

'Got to the settlement in the evening. Managed to get a carcase and sat over it close to a Boma which the lions had raided. No lions came that night. In the morning I made camp some two miles from the village on the banks of the Tana and walked down the river to look for spoor. Saw nothing fresh. Later the scouts arrived to report that the lions had tried to enter another Boma during the night but were driven off. Yesterday evening I again sat up over a carcase in a clearing half a mile from this other Boma. About 11 p.m. without any warning, Little Elsa suddenly appeared and pounced on the carcase which was fastened to a tree stump. She was followed immediately by Jespah, who had an arrow, fortunately not poisoned, sticking in his rump. Both started to eat. Presently I saw Gopa lurking in the distance. Finally he also came to the meat. They were extremely thin and looked starved. They showed no fear when I talked to them and finished off the diminutive goat in an hour. They frequently came up of their own accord to the bowl of water I had placed close to the back of the car. I am confident that they recognised my voice and I am sure that they will come again tonight. There is no doubt that it is the cubs that have been raiding the Bomas. We will have to pay lots of compensation. Send Ibrahim with your Land-Rover at once with all the goats. I must immediately take on a gang of local men to cut a track, and then we will have to move the whole camp and get a lorry here with crates and finally move the cubs out of this district. But the most urgent thing is to send the goats with Ibrahim. If the river is too high, he will have to go the long way round, but he *must* get here today. The cubs are very hungry and will certainly raid another Boma unless I feed them. There is no doubt that all the trouble has been caused by the Fierce Lioness who must have chased the cubs away from Elsa's camp on 4th March.

Yours, G. Please send all my ammunition.'

When I read this I felt as if all my blood were draining away from me. At first I could not get over my surprise at the extraordinary coincidence that a pride with three cubs of the same size as Elsa's should arrive in the area just now and thus deceive us into thinking that Jespah, Gopa and Little Elsa were still around the camp.

Then I remembered the pride to which Elsa, when she herself

was pregnant, had given her goat and acted as aunt. Was it possible that the Fierce Lioness was the mother of these cubs, born perhaps just before Elsa's? It seemed almost certain that the pride, this morning, I had taken to be Elsa's cubs was the family of the Fierce Lioness. This was an anticlimax to the happiness I had felt a few hours earlier. How the cubs had managed to survive on their own for several weeks, I could not imagine. They were too young to know how to hunt wild animals successfully and they must have gone through a ghastly period of starvation before they came upon the goats which they would regard as their natural food. The angry reception from the enraged tribesmen must have terrified them. On the other hand, the tribesmen could not be blamed for defending their stock. The only hope now was to pay heavy compensation and to find a safe place for the family with the least possible delay.

I set off with Ibrahim, with a scout as a guide, five goats and all our essential camping material. We reached the Tana just before dark. The river here was about four hundred yards wide; tall trees grew along the banks and a narrow belt of undergrowth provided the only touch of colour. The flat hinterland covered with dense bush was dry, grey and dusty.

From this point the scout had to guide us on foot over the last eight miles, for the bush was so thick that it was impossible to see any distance ahead or to avoid obstacles. Reconnoitring in the dark he found a way for the car to advance slowly, dodging trees and anti-bear holes, laying bushes flat and crossing deeply eroded river beds, some of which were flooded.

We found the Boma of the headman, but we went on another two miles to George's camp. There we were told that he was sitting up for the cubs. I drove on to join him, arriving at about 9 p.m. George, usually sparing of compliments, greeted me approvingly with: 'How the devil did you manage to get through this bush in the dark?' While we waited for the arrival of the cubs, George told me about Jespah's wound.

A number of tribesmen had set out to kill the lions. They cornered Jespah in the thorn enclosure which protected a flock of goats. The lion had killed two of the goats but before it could get away with its spoils was surrounded by a band of angry tribesmen, armed with bows and poisoned arrows. The lion took cover in the thick thorn fence, and into this the Africans shot about twenty arrows. Luckily the fence was so thick that the arrows did not penetrate. Only one shot loosed by a toto found its mark. Fortunately the arrowhead was not lethal, as the toto was too young to be trusted by his elders with the deadly poison. The arrowhead had luckily not penetrated deeply into Jespah's rump. It did not seem to hinder his movements, nor could it be causing him any pain, since George had often seen him lie on it. The cubs were very friendly and did not object to his presence, but of course there was no question of Jespah allowing him to remove the arrowhead.

George had engaged thirty Africans to cut an eight-mile track along the river; this would enable us to bring up our whole camp in the lorry. He had also taken on four trackers to help with spooring, and had promised very generous compensation to the owners of raided stock.

George suggested that it might be better if I spent the night in camp in case the cubs should turn up there; so after calling 'cu-cu-coo' and their names for a long time but getting no response, I drove back.

Next morning George came back for breakfast; he had seen no sign of the cubs, nor had the game scouts who had been guarding the huts with their thunder-flashes. George then went off spooring with Nuru; he was the only African the cubs knew and his presence was unlikely to make them bolt.

When he returned from his fruitless search we made our plans. George decided to sit up at night inside his Land-Rover on routes which he thought the cubs would take to reach the Bomas; he would have meat placed ready for them. I would do the same at the camp, while the scouts, equipped with thunder-flashes, would protect the various Bomas. Should any of us see the cubs we would warn George by firing shots: one if the scouts sighted them, two if I did.

When it got dark, George left for his vigil, but on this night the cubs took a different route, raided a Boma and mauled a sheep;

32

before they were able to feed they were driven off by the scouts' thunder-flashes.

The next night the cubs tried their luck at yet another Boma and mauled two goats; again before being able to eat they were chased off.

The rains were due to start very soon and we were worried because, when this happened, we would be immobilised if we did not have a four-wheel-drive lorry. We also needed a lorry to bring up our camp kit, to help the labour gang and, above all, for the final move when we had caught the cubs. Indeed, for this we should need two lorries; for we saw the convoy as comprising a lorry for the lions, a lorry for our camp kit and two Land-Rovers to carry our personal luggage.

I decided that I had better go to Isiolo and order a new Bedford lorry on which the three travelling crates, already ordered, could be loaded. Next morning I started off. When I inquired about ordering a new Bedford lorry, I was told that delivery would take about three weeks. This was very inconvenient. So I made the necessary arrangements to hire a truck and I started back in Ken's truck to Elsa's camp to pick up the kit we had left behind and to sleep there. This was the last night I spent in our old camp which had been like a home to me.

We arrived at the new camp the next day about tea-time, and George greeted me with the news that although he had tracked every day and sat up every night he had not once seen the cubs, but each night they had raided a Boma. He was very worried, because in spite of their recent forays, they had, so far as he knew, not eaten for ten days, since they had always been driven away from the Bomas before they could eat their kill. He feared that sooner or later they would injure someone. Their hunting ranged over eight miles of dense bush country. The fact that they never attacked the same Boma on two successive nights made it impossible for George to anticipate their moves. Twice Jespah had even got into a hut. On the first occasion a woman asleep inside with her goats round her was woken by a bleat from her pet billy-goat and saw Jespah's jaws clamp round its throat. She shrieked, and Jespah dropped the goat and made his escape. Undaunted,

33

Jespah on the following night entered a hut occupied by a youth, also surrounded by goats. The boy woke up to find Jespah's rump protruding from under his bed as he tried to rake out a goat which had taken shelter there. The boy yelled and kicked, and Jespah decamped.

That evening about 9 p.m. as George was sitting up over a carcase, he suddenly saw Jespah and Little Elsa. They were terribly emaciated and the arrow was still in Jespah's rump. Neither, however, seemed nervous, and Jespah licked the cod-liver oil out of the pie-dish which George held out to him. They ate ravenously and did not leave till 5 a.m. After this, we thought it likely that Gopa had deserted his brother and sister and that it was his spoor the tracker had seen heading in the direction of the old camp. We therefore sent a runner with instructions to the scouts who were keeping an eye on Elsa's camp to feed Gopa if he turned up, and to let us know if he did.

George spent the rest of the day paying out heavy compensation to the tribesmen; in the evening he waited at a place close to where he thought the cubs were lying-up. It rained all night; the cubs did not appear. Instead, they had gone to the spot where they had seen him the night before, and not finding him there had raided three Bomas, killed two goats and mauled six others.

Later a scout arrived from Elsa's camp and reported that during the night a young lion had been there and had left his pug marks all over the place where George usually pitched his tent; afterwards he had gone off towards the Big Rock. On the follow-ing night he had returned in the company of a big lion. The young lion had gone first to the tree we used as a 'bush-fridge,' then to Elsa's grave and finally into the old crate. This confirmed our belief that it must be Gopa. No doubt disgusted at being chased out of the Bomas before he could get a meal, hunger had prevailed over his natural timidity and he had made the journey home on his own, hoping to find us in camp with a square meal ready for him.

Since the two scouts who were over at the camp were unfamiliar with the cubs' habits we sent Nuru back to feed Gopa. As soon as it was possible to cross the flooded river by car, I intended to join him. If Gopa were to act as a guide to the other cubs and induce them to return to Elsa's camp, this would greatly facilitate our task. But unless and until this happened our problem would be even greater than before Gopa's departure. It had been difficult enough to follow the cub's movements, and try to prevent them from carrying out their raids when they were all together, but trying to control two danger areas fourteen miles apart, at a time when rain made movement by car nearly impossible, was a nightmare.

That night the cubs passed within a hundred yards of George on their way from a Boma where they had eaten part of a dead goat which the tribesmen had thrown out. We were desperate. All we could do was to reinforce the thorn enclosures around all the Bomas and set scouts to guard as many of them as possible; but there were not enough scouts to go round.

5 THE CAPTURE

George had spent night after night sitting up in the most appalling conditions, and each day had gone out in search of the cubs, but he found no sign of them. But one night, as he sat up in my car with a meal ready, Jespah and Little Elsa arrived, ate ravenously and stayed till 11 p.m. In the early hours of the morning George heard both cubs roaring. We wondered whether they were calling to Gopa – or asserting their right to their new territory.

On the following night the two cubs came in early, ate half the meal George had prepared for them, and then, when it started to rain, went off and apparently out of sheer devilment attacked a Boma, killing three goats and mauling four more.

The next evening, he found Jespah and Little Elsa waiting for him, and for some time he sat in the dark and heard them contentedly eating the meal he had provided. Later, when he switched on his headlights, he was surprised to see three cubs. Gopa must just have arrived, for he was formally greeting his brother and sister. He must have been very hungry, but looked fit. He had been away for over a week. All the cubs took their cod-liver oil, after which they went off in the direction of the Bomas. George fired a warning shot, so the scouts were on the alert when the cubs arrived and greeted them with thunder-flashes which scared them off.

Day by day now the weather was getting worse, and it was vital that we should be completely prepared for the capture and get the crates up before the rain made transport by lorry impossible. The fourteen-mile track through the bush to Elsa's camp had now been cut.

So to collect all the things we required, I set off with Ibrahim for Isiolo. We had great difficulty in crossing the river even at the narrow ford.

While at Isiolo I heard from Major Grimwood that he had

obtained permission for us to take the cubs to the Serengeti National Park in Tanganyika. I was extremely pleased, for the Serengeti is famous for lions and an abundance of game; I felt that we could not have found a better home for Elsa's cubs.

There was much to do at Isiolo. Having got the truck problem settled, I speeded up the completion of the three box-traps, ordered pulleys, ropes, car-batteries and photographic materials.

It rained without stopping and I itched to get back before we were cut off by the floods. When I finally arrived, complete with three crates and the lorry, George told me that the cubs had come to him during each of the four nights I had been absent, and that though they had tried to make some raids they had been driven off.

The cubs were now in excellent condition. Jespah still carried the arrowhead in his rump, but it did not appear to cause him any discomfort or interfere with his movements. They had recovered their trust in George and were quite at ease as he walked among them while they fed, refilling their water bowl and their pie-dishes of cod-liver oil.

This was certainly an improvement, but we still felt as though we were living on a volcano. True, the cubs, even when desperately hungry and driven off their kills, had never attempted to injure anyone; true, the tribesmen had shown great patience and been very helpful – indeed, they seemed well pleased with their compensation and the ready market provided for their surplus goats – none the less it was worrying to reflect that the bush all round us was swarming with herds of goats and sheep and that these herds were in the charge of small children. The sooner the cubs were captured and removed the better for everybody.

To this end, we cleared an opening in the bush close to the place where they were in the habit of lying-up during the day. There we placed the three crates side by side and George rigged up an ingenious trapdoor arrangement.

The first thing to do was to accustom the cubs to feed in the crates, and then wait for the critical moment. For eleven nights now they had come more or less regularly to be fed by George, so to entice them from the vicinity of the Bomas and in the direction of the traps, he gradually moved the place at which he fed them towards the crates. When he had lured the cubs to within a quarter of a mile of them he attached two carcases to the Land-Rover and when the cubs appeared slowly towed the meat towards the box-traps. Jespah promptly foiled his scheme by swinging a carcase round a tree-trunk causing the rope to break. On the next night George had better luck, for the cubs followed their dinner right up to the crates. They did not show any fear of the large boxes – Gopa even sat inside one of them while he ate his meal.

At last it looked as though we might capture the cubs fairly soon. This was a great relief, but George felt that if we were to successfully carry out our move to the Serengeti, he must resign from his job so that he could devote his time exclusively to the cubs. I knew how this decision pained George.

I returned once again to Isiolo to pick up the communal crate and as many goats as possible.

On my way back to camp we were halted by torrential flooding and had to send two scouts across country to bring back the Land-Rover. We settled down to wait for our rescue party and I began to read the mail I had collected in Isiolo but had not yet opened. In it I found a collection of newspaper cuttings with the most terrifying headlines:

'Elsa's cubs may, have to be shot.'
'Death threats to Elsa's cubs.'
'Elsa's cubs: sentence of death.'

I was terrified. I knew, of course, that if the cubs scratched anyone, even slightly, they would be sentenced to death; mercifully they had not done so, but it was vital to move them as soon as possible, and meanwhile we had to remain inactive, facing the unfordable river.

Suddenly the rain stopped. Ibrahim and I anxiously watched the water slowly subsiding. As I feared that the scouts, making their way on foot to the camp, might have been delayed, I suggested that Julian McKeand, who had come with me from Isiolo to help in the capture, should drive as near to the camp as he could, taking Ibrahim with him so that when they could go no farther in the Land-Rover Ibrahim could walk the rest of the way and deliver my message to George.

They set off, and after the car had reached its limit, Ibrahim plodded for many miles waist-deep through slush and, as I expected, reached the camp long before the scouts turned up. George sent Ibrahim back to us in his Land-Rover, and at noon the next day we saw him waving cheerfully to us from the opposite bank.

Soon after our arrival in camp, George took us to see the box-traps and demonstrated his device. We were all very much impressed when, as soon as he released the rope, the three doors crashed down simultaneously like guillotines.

He told us that the cubs had come every night and that each had entered a crate to eat the meat he had placed in it. Jespah had even spent a whole night inside one of them. The trouble was that sometimes two cubs would go into the same box; or if all three were in different crates, then a head or a rump would protrude beyond the door, making it impossible to use the guillotine device. Would they ever, all three, be at the same time in a position which would make it possible for us to capture them?

Soon after dark the cubs arrived for their meal, and spent the whole night close to the car.

Next morning Julian drove back to Isiolo, intending to return with the new Bedford truck as soon as it was delivered. We hoped that his arrival might coincide with the capture of the cubs. When that happened he would be of great assistance to us, for we were very short-handed.

We were full of hope that our anxieties might be nearing an end when the mail brought us a bombshell. George received a letter from the District Commissioner in whose area we now stayed, containing an ultimatum to capture the cubs within a stated period. He was sorry to have to give this order, but since the situation was being exploited politically he could not give us his support after this date.

We were most distressed; for although we believed that we were nearing the time when we might hope to capture the cubs, we were

39

working under great handicaps. The one satisfactory thing was that for the last nine days the cubs had stopped raiding Bomas and had come every night to George for their food.

It was the 24th April. I had not seen them since the 27th February, when Jespah had played with me on the Whuffing Rock. In the hope of seeing them again I joined George and after parking my car close to his, I prepared lumps of meat in which I concealed doses of terramycin and placed them inside the crates with the carcases. Then we waited inside our Land-Rovers.

Soon after dark I felt something brush against my car – it was Jespah. Silently he went straight to the crates. He ate two of the titbits containing terramycin and then walked over to George, who was standing outside his car holding out a pie-dish of cod-liver oil. The cub licked it clean and then returned to his dinner. He showed no surprise at seeing me, and had grown enormously and filled out.

Suddenly I heard a rustling in a bush behind my car and, flashing my torch, caught a glimpse of Gopa, some twenty yards away. For a quarter of an hour he remained there in hiding, then he was joined by Little Elsa. I called 'Cu-cu-coo' to them, but so far from encouraging them, this caused Gopa to bolt twice, but in the end he could not resist the smell of the meat and cautiously sneaked up to the crates. He ate the lumps of meat and cleared out both pie-dishes of cod-liver oil before he started on the carcase. Little Elsa was extremely shy, and it was long after midnight before she ventured to approach the crates. By then all the terramycin and the cod-liver oil had been eaten by her brothers.

All the cubs were in good condition. Having seen the photographs George had taken of them when he had first found them on the Tana, which showed them as pathetic skeletons, I realised what an incredible job he had done. That they were now in splendid health and that their trust in us had been restored was entirely due to his patience and ingenuity. We watched them eating until 4 a.m. when they departed with heavy bellies.

Several evenings later all three cubs arrived again. Soon afterwards a lion roared, but they paid no attention to him. Jespah and Little Elsa were inside separate crates, busy with their dinner.

Gopa visited them in turn, but finding himself unwelcome, sat down sulkily at the entrance to the third crate. Would he enter it? Should we be able to release the trapdoors and capture the cubs? The suspense was nerve-racking and increased by our fear that the lion we had recently heard might in time induce the cubs to follow him. If they did we should be unable to protect them from the death warrant or from the tribesmen's arrows.

The following night we again had cause to worry for at the first roar the cubs stopped eating, listened intently, dropped the meat and rushed off in the direction from which the calls came. They all returned later to finish their meal; but we could not help wondering whether they would always come back.

Ibrahim returned from Isiolo with the news that the new Bedford would not be ready for ten days. This was inconvenient, and it also meant that Julian would not come back to help us. Another new worry was that whenever heavy rains fell – and they fell frequently – the roads were now to be officially closed to traffic.

Meanwhile our trackers had come in and reported that the cubs' spoor led in the direction of the wild lion. If we waited for the weather to improve and for the Bedford to arrive when the roads were reopened, the cubs might well by then have wandered off with the local lion and run into disaster.

We spent the day improving the trapping device and rehearsing our parts in the capture. In spite of these occupations the hours seemed to drag until it was time to sit up for the cubs.

I had barely finished putting the terramycin into the meat lumps when Jespah appeared. He ate two of them and then came and sat in front of our cars and watched us. Meanwhile his brother and sister entered separate crates. A little later they came out and lay near Jespah. They looked very lovely in the bright moonlight and I longed to remove them from the dangers which were increasing. But as if to mock me, the lion chose this moment to roar, and the cubs went off like a flash. I heard a hearty curse from George's car; another of the few remaining nights was lost. Resigned, I went to lie on my bed, asking George to call me when it was my turn to keep watch, or before that, if anything should happen. I felt very depressed but was so tired that I dozed off.

Suddenly I was woken by the crashing of the crate doors. A deathly silence followed; it was as if all life had suddenly stopped. After a short time the struggle inside the crates began. Simultaneously George and I ran to them, quickly removed the wooden blocks we had placed below the doors to prevent any damage to protruding tails, and closed the narrow slits so as to remove any opportunity for leverage and make an attempt to escape impossible.

Although it was an immense relief to know that the cubs were now safe, both George and I felt disgusted at the deception we had practised on them.

6 THE JOURNEY TO THE SERENGETI

Now there was no time to lose if we wished to reduce the cubs' time of discomfort and bewilderment to a minimum. George remained on guard and I went back to camp, woke the men, told them the news, then, together, we hurriedly packed up, so as to be ready to hoist the cubs on to the truck at first light.

When all was ready we drove the five-ton Bedford to the crates. George told me that after Jespah had recovered from the shock of finding himself trapped, he had calmed down and spent most of the night sitting quietly in his box. Little Elsa had followed his example, but Gopa had gone on fighting for a long time. Now he was growling savagely at our boys, who had come to help in hoisting the crates on to the truck.

Although we had told the tribesmen not to come near the lions, a chattering crowd soon collected. This terrified Gopa, who in his struggle broke one of the ceiling planks of his cage and split two others. We immediately covered the gap with a ground sheet, fixed iron bars across it and tied them on with thick ropes. Then we hoisted the crates, each of which weighed well over 800 lb. As the heavy boxes, lifted by block and tackle dangled in the air, the horrified lions paced to and fro, causing the crates to sway alarmingly. We hoisted Little Elsa first; Gopa we placed alongside her, Jespah's crate we placed broadside across the end of the lorry. In this way the cubs had the fullest view of each other. It also had the advantage of making it possible to get at Jespah from the rear of the truck, so that we could try to extract his arrowhead as soon as an opportunity arose.

We were ready to move; leaving the jabbering crowd behind, we proceeded in convoy. The first fourteen miles were very rough, the trucks bumping over boulders as they wound their way through dense shrub along the newly-cut track. In spite of the shaking, the cubs lay down and took the drive well.

We found the river still in flood, but just fordable. Heavy rain clouds were gathering on every side; we were surrounded by a threatening black wall. Skidding through mud, we raced this colossal storm for sixty miles and won only by a hair's breadth.

At dusk when we passed the boundary of the district I took a very deep breath: the cubs were now outside the jurisdiction of the death sentence. Altogether we had more than seven hundred miles to travel. From now on most of the way lay through highlands which rose to 7,500 feet. We had started at an elevation of 1,200 feet, and had now reached an altitude of 7,000 feet. It was bitterly cold. Above us, Mount Kenya's ragged, ice-covered peaks rose to 17,000 feet; they were covered with heavy cloud and drizzling rain fell upon us as we went along its base.

The weather got worse, the drizzling rain turned to a real downpour and it became icy cold. We stopped often to fasten the flapping tarpaulins to the cubs' lorry, and I felt very sorry for them crouching in the farthest corners trying to avoid the drenching rain. All through the night we were at an altitude of 5,000 feet, and I feared they might develop pneumonia.

We reached Nairobi at 3 a.m. and filled up the tanks. The hours between 3 a.m. and daylight were a great strain on all of us. As we crossed the Kajiado Plain there were gusts of icy wind and several cloudbursts. Our drivers were worn out by their efforts to keep their vehicles on the slippery road. This part of the journey must have been torture to the cubs.

Dawn found us a few miles short of Namanga, close to the Tanganyika border. The cubs were completely exhausted and lay apathetically in their cages, their faces chafed by the constant friction against the bars. We gave them fresh meat and water, in which they showed no interest.

To reduce the length of their misery as much as we could we decided that I should drive full speed ahead to Arusha, a hundred miles distant, announce our arrival to the Director of the National Parks, and find out the location of the release point in the Serengeti. George would follow with the cubs at a slower pace and we would meet at a short distance outside the town, where we should avoid a crowd of curious spectators.

As soon as I entered Arusha, I went to see the Director of the National Parks to discuss the locality of the release point.

He agreed that we might take the cubs to an area near a river which never went dry. He very kindly promised to send a radio message to one of the park wardens asking him to meet us on our way and guide us to this spot.

After leaving the director it took me five hours' driving to find George who had driven the lorry 60 miles beyond Arusha. As the next stage of our journey was through highlands where it was bound to be very cold, we thought it would be unwise to continue, so we stopped.

The cubs were in a pitiful state. Their faces were bruised and battered and the bony parts of their bodies were chafed; the decomposing meat inside the crates attracted a swarm of blue-bottles which buzzed over their sores. They tried unsuccessfully to protect themselves by putting their paws over their faces; I could not bear to watch their suffering.

The next morning we began to climb up the escarpment which towered above us. Concentrating on speed, we climbed steadily into the 'Highlands of the Giant Volcanoes'. The higher we climbed, the thicker the fog grew and it began to penetrate icily through our clothes. At last we reached the rim of the Ngorongoro crater. On an earlier visit, I had looked down it and seen a multitude of game grazing some 1,500 feet below, but today nothing was visible but billowing clouds. For a few miles we crawled cautiously along the slippery road round the rim, then, all of a sudden, the mist lifted; it was as though a curtain had suddenly been raised on a new scene and we saw, far below us, the Serengeti Plain bathed in warm sunlight.

Ahead of us lay undulating slopes, covered with great herds of zebra, wildebeest, Thomson's gazelle and cattle herded by Masai tribesmen. It was strange to see wild and domestic animals feeding side by side.

We came down rapidly to an altitude of 5,000 feet, at which level the sun was so warm that we were able to shed some of our clothes. We now had only some seventy miles to go. The road had been fair so far; suddenly it deteriorated into one of the worst tracks we had ever travelled over. As the heat increased we removed the tarpaulins which covered the lorry, to prevent the cubs from suffocating, but this resulted in their raw wounds being covered with dust; they were indeed having a terrible time for they were bounced about mercilessly as the lorry lurched from one pothole to another. I did not know which was worse for the cubs, the icy wet and cold we had just left behind, or the infernal heat and appalling dust of the next fifty miles. We were two hours late when we reached Naabi Hill at which we were to meet the park warden.

Now we had to cut our greetings short, for heavy storm clouds were gathering and we still had a long way to go through black cotton soil, the worst ground to cross when wet. Dodging between the herds and avoiding swampy patches we reached the release point in the late afternoon.

7 THE RELEASE

The cubs' new home was a very beautiful place lying at the head of a broad valley some forty miles long. On one side, a steep escarpment rose to a plateau, on the other, there was a succession of hills. Close by, was a river which gradually wound its way to the centre of the valley and flowed down it. Its banks were covered with dense undergrowth and fine trees, which provided perfect cover for all kinds of animals. But for the mosquitoes and tsetse flies, it was a paradise – and perhaps we ought to have regarded the tsetse as its winged guardians, for they are the best protectors of wild animals: since they are fatal to men and to their livestock, they cause them to keep away.

Our first thought was to see what we could do to make the cubs more comfortable. We chose a stout acacia tree, attached the block and tackle to one of its branches, and swung the crates to the ground. It was three days since the cubs had been captured and they had almost reached the limit of their endurance. Their eyes were deeply sunken and they lay apathetically on the floor of their cages, apparently too tired to take the least interest in their surroundings. How glad we were that we had decided to bring the cumbersome communal crate. It had no floor, could easily be moved to fresh ground, and would provide the lions with a spacious and comfortable place of confinement in which they would be able to recover from the strain of their journey.

After opening the back of the communal crate, we placed Little Elsa's and Gopa's boxes with their doors opposite the opening, then with block and tackle we raised the trapdoors of the cages.

For a few moments nothing happened, then, suddenly, Gopa rushed into Little Elsa's box; he sat on her and they licked and hugged each other, overwhelmed with joy at being reunited. Quickly we closed the door behind them and replaced Gopa's

47

empty crate by the one containing Jespah. The instant we opened his door he was out like a flash, and covered his brother and sister, as if to protect them from further disaster and started to lick and embrace them.

We were delighted to see that in spite of all they had gone through the cubs were as friendly as they had always been. Now we had to see that they got rested and made up for their lost meals. We put a carcase into the communal crate, and parked our Land-Rovers right and left of the crate to protect the cubs from any prowlers that might come by night. By 9 p.m. all this had been done, and we were ready for a good sleep.

Next morning I was glad to see that there was nothing left of the meal we had prepared the night before. The cubs had gone back into the filthy travelling crates; they seemed to cling to them as the one familiar place which gave them a sense of security in their strange surroundings. Until they became less bewildered it was plain that we must keep them confined; to entice them into the communal crate we put some fresh meat into it. We thought it very important to leave them undisturbed, so we gave strict orders to our staff to keep away from the crates, and we ourselves went to find a camping site at least a mile away.

The park warden and his family came to discuss our camping arrangements. The park authorities had kindly given us permission to look after the cubs until they had settled in their new home and could fend for themselves. The park warden told us that we could feed them on game animals shot outside the Serengeti Park, specified the area, which was some 40 miles away, and also the type of animal we were allowed to shoot.

When we got back to the cubs we found all three in the communal crate. Their faces were a shocking sight, for the big cage was made of weld-mesh wire which chafed them even more than the iron bars of the travelling crates. Every time they pressed against it their wounds reopened, and they made matters worse by using their paws to try and keep the flies off their sores. Poor Gopa was the most battered and he and Little Elsa growled savagely whenever we came close to the crate. Jespah did not mind our

48

Jespah, Gopa and Little Elsa just after
their first birthday

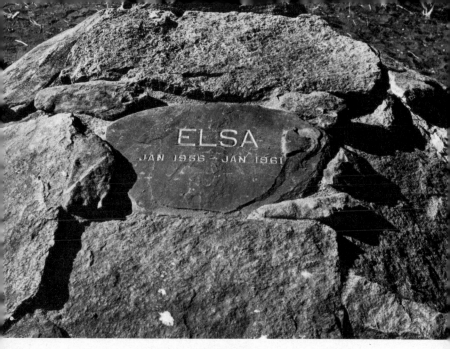

Elsa's grave

Jespah and Joy exchange opinions!

The cubs were like skeletons when George found them on the Tana

George checks the final details of his trapping device

A wary, but hungry cub eyes his dinner

Caged

'We hoisted the crates, each of which weighed
well over 800 lb.'

'Jespah's expression was almost unendurable'

Jespah had carried
the arrowhead for
five weeks now

A rest at the
journey's end

Jespah surveys the Serengeti

A leopard in the Serengeti

Zebra: just a few taking part in the vast migration

The tallest inhabitant of the park

A pride claims right of way

This herd was part of the migration

Joy and Jespah a
few days before the
cubs finally disappear

A view from the
heights

Forever Free

presence and even allowed us to pluck at the arrowhead; but we failed to extract it.

We settled down for the night, the communal cage sheltered between our two cars; soon afterwards we heard the first lion approaching. The whuffing came rapidly nearer, until we could distinguish several animals circling round our little sanctuary – and then saw their eyes reflecting the light of our torches. The cubs listened intently to their grunts, while we shouted at them trying to shoo them away. When all was quiet again, I called the cubs softly by their names, and soon afterwards heard them tearing at their meat.

After breakfast the next morning George drove off to shoot a 'kill' outside the Serengeti while I remained with the cubs. Whenever Jespah gave me an opportunity to do so I tried to remove the arrow from his rump. He did not mind even when I pinched the skin and tugged as hard as I could, but the barb remained jammed. Jespah had been hit five weeks ago and I did not like the look of the wound; but as the vet had advised against operating for a few more weeks, I had to resign myself to waiting.

Later in the morning the plague of flies made the cubs very restless; they paced up and down, rubbing their heads against the wire and reopening their wounds, but in the end cuddled up together, looking at me reproachfully. In spite of being caged, dirty and covered with bleeding wounds, they were as dignified as only lions could be under such conditions.

I knew that the Serengeti was far the best home we could have found for them, but the climate and the ecological conditions were very different from those of their old home and most of the local animals belonged to species unknown to them. Even the local lions were of a different sub-species from theirs. What would their mutual reactions be and what trouble might arise over territorial rights?

When George returned about 3 o'clock with a carcase we discussed the question of releasing the cubs. We had intended to keep them confined for another day or two so as to build them up, but the torment of the flies made us change our minds and we decided to release them then and there.

It was a good time of day, since during the hot hours the cubs were less energetic, therefore less likely to bolt or panic; moreover, at this hour there was less danger of their meeting wild lions. After placing the carcase between the cage and the river, we hoisted one of the travelling boxes, thus opening an exit. When they saw us doing this the cubs rushed in terror to the farthest corners of the communal crate and huddled close together. After some time, Gopa suspiciously investigated the opening, cautiously retreated several times, and then walked out in a most dignified manner. He took no interest in the 'kill' but continued slowly towards the river. After about a hundred yards he stopped, hesitated, and then walked calmly on.

Jespah and Little Elsa held each other close; they had puzzled expressions as they watched Gopa walking away. Then Jespah went up to the exit and moved out. He too went very slowly towards the river, pausing several times to look back at his sister.

Meanwhile Little Elsa rushed frantically up and down the crate or stood upright against it, plainly desperately anxious to join her brothers and not knowing how to do so, till at last she found the way to freedom and trotted quickly after Jespah, and all three cubs disappeared into the reeds. Almost immediately a cloudburst screened them from our view.

8 THE MIGRATION

As soon as the grey curtain lifted we searched the place where we had last seen the cubs through our field-glasses but there was no trace of them. I was glad that at least they had walked straight to the river, since this meant that they would know where to get a drink.

One of our first tasks would be to find a feeding place, where the cubs could eat without the local lions or other predators interfering with them. To secure their meat inside the communal crate would be risky, for in a confined space the cubs might be cornered. What we needed was a shelter for the 'kill' which provided an easy exit for the cubs in case of danger. We placed the communal crate near a large tree; on either side we parked our two cars, thus making an open square. Across a thick branch we hoisted the 'kill' by a block and tackle. We did not expect the cubs that night, for until they were hungry we did not think they would return to the crates in which they had been trapped.

Soon after dark a pride of three or more lions came so close that the light from our torches was reflected in their eyes. They were followed by a few hyenas. A little later we heard baboons shrieking alarm, and sweeping our spotlight in the direction from which the noise came saw three pairs of eyes, halfway up the hill beyond the river. We thought these might be those of the cubs who, after their experience with the Fierce Lioness, were likely to keep away from other lions.

To discourage the wild pride from coming to get a free meal, we spent most of the night scaring them away. It was easy to know when the lion was around for he always announced his arrival by a low grunt, but the lionesses sneaked in silently and I only became aware of them when I heard their breathing and by then they were crouching by my car. However, in spite of their cunning they never got at the 'kill.'

Early next morning we spotted the cubs coming out of the bush, very close to the place at which they had disappeared the night before. They walked half-way up the hill, stopping often, until they reached a thicket; there they lay down. When I called to them they looked at me but did not move.

Next evening the cubs arrived at about 9 p.m. They ate hungrily and Jespah even asked for two rations of cod-liver oil taking it in his usual way out of the pie-dish which George held out to him, so we knew that in spite of all he had lately suffered he still trusted us.

We spent the next day reconnoitring the area. The annual migration of the animals of the plain was expected to move through the valley soon, but, although the day before George had seen some large herds of wildebeeste and zebra assembling near the border, today we saw only the usual inhabitants of the valley: herds of impala, topi, waterbuck and kongoni and some solitary bushbuck and reedbuck and later, as we went farther down the valley, many buffalo and a few elephant.

Towards evening we went back to our post near the 'kill'. Gopa arrived at dusk, but hid in the tall grass until he thought it was dark enough to be safe for him to come to his meal. Jespah soon followed him, but Little Elsa did not appear. Instead, a dark-maned lion and his two lionesses turned up. They crouched within eight yards of my car while, on the other side of it, Gopa and Jespah crunched their dinner. Jespah and Gopa were not in the least worried by the proximity of the local lions, indeed, they must have felt perfectly safe and have had complete confidence in our ability to protect them, for when they were full up they rolled on their backs.

Suddenly there was a faint call from over the river; perhaps it was Little Elsa for instantly the brothers sneaked off behind George's car, avoiding the wild lions. We hoisted the 'kill' and spent the rest of the night keeping the wild pride at bay.

On the 7th of May, George left early to get a new 'kill' outside the Serengeti. A Land-Rover unexpectedly appeared, bringing the Chairman of the Trustees of the National Park and his party, which included the park warden. The chairman told me that he appreciated the publicity the cubs were giving to the Serengeti, but went on to say that by the end of May we must leave, as the tourist season opened in June and our camping out and feeding the lions might arouse criticism. I was horrified, for we had brought the cubs to the Serengeti believing that we should be allowed to look after them until they were able to provide for themselves, and no one could yet tell when that would be. I told the chairman that we had always wished to ensure that the cubs should eventually lead a wild life, and that for this reason we had refrained from making pets of them; but I stressed that we really could not abandon them until they were able to fend for themselves. I suggested, to avoid the difficulties he foresaw, that we should move our camp to some place far from the tourist tracks, and I promised to be very discreet about feeding the cubs, but pointed out that by the end of May they would only be seventeen months old and that as a rule lions of that age are not yet able to hunt on their own.

At this moment George returned, and supported my view. The chairman did not agree to our proposal and left us dismayed. The cubs had only been released a few days; up till then they had been dependent upon us, and we felt it would be monstrous just to dump them and hope that they would manage somehow.

When we took up our night station we found the cubs already waiting for us. Jespah came several times to the back of my car asking to be patted and remained quite still while I stroked him. This was the first time he had done such a thing since he had left Elsa's camp. In spite of all that had happened, perhaps because of his mother's example, he still trusted us and acted as liaison between his brother and sister and ourselves. We were both sure that without him neither Gopa nor Little Elsa would have put up with us. Gopa had the strength and independence to be the leader of a pride, but he lacked the qualities of affection and understanding which distinguished his mother and his brother. Although it was Gopa who left the Tana, made his way back to his old home and spent a week there on his own; although he was the one to fight most fiercely when he was trapped and who first took the risk of making his way to freedom out of the communal crate and claimed the lion's share of every meal – yet, when he was distressed or frightened, Gopa at once rushed to Jespah for comfort and support, as he used to rush to his mother.

Jespah appeared to provide the moral backbone for the trio, which was probably what caused him to become the leader, even though he was less powerful than Gopa. From a very early age he had always protected his mother and since her death he had taken charge of his brother and sister. It was always he who went out to reconnoitre and see if there was danger around, and if a threat arose it was he who challenged it, and recently whenever Little Elsa bolted he had run after her, comforted her and brought her back.

The cubs spent the night devouring the fresh 'kill'. At dawn they walked off, their bellies swinging heavily from side to side. They were in perfect condition, except for some sores from chafing, and of course Jespah still had the arrowhead in his rump.

During the next two nights only the three local lions and a few hyena came to the 'kill'. One of these was particularly cunning. He waited beyond the range of our headlights until we were no longer on the alert and then dashed up to the meat.

There was no sign of the cubs so George went off alone to search for them. He found their spoor leading across the valley towards the escarpment, where rocks offered them good shelter. We thought that they probably felt safer at a distance from the local lions, even if this meant that they had to walk two miles to get their dinner.

One afternoon we drove across the plain to look at some rocky outcrops which provided ideal lie-ups for lions. As we passed some rocks we saw a pride of lions, who sleepily observed our approach but soon lost interest in us and continued their siesta. The tawny heap consisted of three lionesses and five cubs. Two of the cubs could not have been more than three weeks old; the others were about the same age as Elsa's cubs. Young lions are most endearing for they still retain the puzzled inquisitive expression of small cubs, while they already have the dignity and stateliness of adult lions.

Two of the lionesses were obviously the mothers of the cubs; the third we assumed to be the traditional 'aunt'. Tumbling clumsily over the bodies of their elders, the two tiny cubs dominated the scene. One, struggling up towards its mother's shoulders, miaouwed in protest when it got stuck, then clambered on, only to roll over and land on Auntie's back, from which vantage point it seized the black tassel at the end of her tail. A quick flick sent it scurrying up her neck, till it found two ears, which it started to chew. But no aunt, however tolerant, could be expected to put up with such impertinence, and this one, shaking her massive head, sent the little cub flying. Hurriedly it scrambled over to its mother, pressing itself against her soft belly, suckling for all it was worth.

Looking at the older cubs, I wished that Elsa's could join such a happy family, but I feared that they were already too big to be adopted by a pride; on the other hand, they might be at a good age to start off on their own life.

That night the cubs arrived soon after our vigil had begun. They seemed unusually nervous and bolted the moment they heard a lion calling, even though he was far away. They did not return till three in the morning, then gulped their food and left. We appreciated the reason for the hurry when soon afterwards a chorus of lions started to roar quite close to us.

It rained all the next day and we went early to the 'kill'. When we reached it we saw Jespah balancing on the branch from which his dinner was hanging; he was trying to get at it from above, while the other cubs, half hidden in the grass, watched him. As soon as we lowered the carcase they all rushed at the meat and spent the night gorging. By morning there was nothing left but a few bones; this meant that we must again drive outside the Serengeti and go hunting for them.

Quite close to the camp we passed the dark-maned lion and his two girl friends. Not more than a mile farther on we saw a magnificent blond-maned lion sunning himself on the open plain. He paid no attention to us or to the clicking of our cameras and stretched and yawned as though we weren't there.

In whatever direction we looked we saw animals chasing and fighting each other. The cheeky little Thomson's gazelle not only challenged each other to a game, but even our Land-Rover. At our approach they stamped their forelegs, but did not move away until we nearly bumped into them. Then eland-antelopes, larger than bulls, bounded away so gracefully that one could have imagined that their heavy bodies were weightless.

The farther we drove, the more wooded and hilly the country became and the more the herds of animals increased. Mile after mile under every tree groups of wildebeeste and zebra crowded together to the limit of the shade; while, in the blazing sun, animals unable to find shelter wandered about aimlessly. The noise was deafening. We were among thousands upon thousands of animals assembled in preparation for their great annual migration towards Lake Victoria and the adjoining Mara Reserve. We were very lucky to have arrived in the Serengeti in time to see this unique sight.

During the next three nights the cubs failed to turn up, but hungry predators were very active. A leopard climbed the acacia tree in an attempt to get at the meat; a bold hyena also tried his luck, and several lions came to investigate the 'kill'. In particular, the dark-maned lion and his pride remained close and were plainly not prepared to allow the cubs to take over their territory.

This made us realise that we must establish a new feeding place for the cubs – but first we had to find them. We spent the next days scouring the country, but the long grass and dry ground made spooring difficult. Besides this, there were so many lions in the valley that it was impossible to identify the cubs' pug marks.

We had never seen so many lions: we walked past a pride of five sitting on a rock, and a short distance away from them we saw a pride of seven lying on a hillock, who looked us up and down but didn't move, even when we had to pass within four yards of them. As we went on we came upon a third pride consisting of a lioness, two small cubs, two half-grown cubs and two magnificent lions, and only a short distance away two dark-maned lions were stalking a topi up a hill.

When the cubs had been missing for six days we became anxious. We had expected them to become independent only gradually, and this sudden disappearance didn't seem natural. We wondered whether they might share the homing instinct with cats. If so, they might now be travelling to their old home – 400 miles if they went in a straight line; 700 if they followed the route by which they had come. That they should follow the road seemed unlikely, but we decided to investigate it and drove back thirty miles to the hill, to where we had first met the park warden. We saw no sign of the cubs. On our way we passed through vast herds of migrating animals and saw one column three miles long of Thomson's gazelle walking in single file, advancing as if drawn by a magnet. In spite of the easy hunting, we did not think it probable that the cubs would have gone into this country, for the open plain offered no shelter and they were used to thick bush cover. All the same, we made a careful search in the rocks and vegetation of the hill before we gave up and returned to camp.

The next morning we took a map and drew a straight line between the Serengeti and Elsa's camp. We passed through some country where there was plenty of cover, but also plenty of lions. We saw a pride of fifteen lying under a tree. Two males with splendid manes watched over their families, consisting of five lionesses who were suckling eight cubs of varying ages. The cubs went from one mother to the other, and the lionesses showed no wish to distinguish between their own cubs and the others.

It was late afternoon when we reached the border without a sign of the cubs. As soon as we got back to the camp I packed, to be ready for an early search the next morning; then I went to the cubs' feeding place to spend the night there in case they might come. Since we had so little time left, George decided to start searching the valley at once. Next morning he arrived grinning; he had found the cubs, or rather they had found him.

He had driven six miles down the valley and parked the car where the headlights could be seen over a great distance. About 9 p.m. the cubs arrived. They looked fit and were not hungry, but they were so thirsty that the brothers lapped up all the water George could give them, leaving nothing for poor Little Elsa. All were very friendly and Jespah even tried to enter George's car. They remained there through the night, eating little of the very high meat he had brought them but amusing themselves by chasing hyenas. When, soon after dawn, they left, they went towards a little valley. George had hurried back to bring me the good news. It was obvious that, after their experience with the Fierce Lioness at Elsa's camp, the cubs were scared of all the lions round the release place and had gone to find a more secluded area where they could stake out their own territory.

We decided not to move the main camp but to go every evening to the 'cub valley' and spend the night there in our cars. The glen they had chosen for their home was at the foot of the escarpment and above the tsetse belt; it provided a particularly safe refuge. It was about half a mile long, its vertical walls were nine feet high and it was five feet wide; above it almost impenetrable vegetation provided a thick canopy which turned it into a cool shelter during the hot hours of the day.

Any approaching danger could be heard from a long way off, so, if need be, the cubs could retreat inside the ravine and up one of the sheer cliffs which broke off the escarpment. Here among over-hanging rocks and dense undergrowth they would be in a strong strategic position to sight and avoid an enemy. We thought that the cubs had found a much better home for themselves than the one we had chosen for them.

When we first arrived at their valley it was late afternoon, we took up our post under a large tree between the escarpment and the river and hoisted up the meat. One cub soon emerged from the ravine but hid in the grass. When it grew dark all three appeared. We observed that all three were in good condition, and the sores due to the chafing were healing well. The arrowhead in Jespah's rump, however, showed no sign of coming out and though he drank his cod-liver oil from the pie-dish I held out to him he would not allow me to pull at the arrow.

9 THE RAVINE

Next day we went to have another look at the migration; it was a truly fantastic sight. The migrating herds spend several weeks assembling; during this time they churn up the plain and after a couple of days the three-foot high grass is reduced to bare stalks of only about four inches. The actual move lasts only a few days and its drive and urgency is something which has to be seen to be believed. What mysterious force suddenly informs these usually placid animals and causes them to move as if at a command? Can it be only a search for water and for better pasturing? Surely some deeper atavism inherited perhaps from bygone ages must be responsible for the phenomenon.

We watched in amazement the herds advancing in tens of thousands and sometimes had the impression that it was the ground itself that was moving. The wildebeeste kept in groups of ten to one hundred or walked in single file along well trodden paths, the zebra, whenever possible, kept close to the water; these two species predominated, but there were also great herds of Thomson's gazelles, also many smaller ones of Grant's gazelles, kongoni and topi, and we counted one herd of two hundred eland-antelopes. On the periphery of the herds were hungry jackals and hyenas watching for the chance to pick up a straggler. In whatever direction we looked the plain was covered with animals whose number it was impossible to estimate.

During the cool hours they were full of energy. We were particularly amused by the behaviour of the shaggy wildebeeste. The bulls chased any of their cows which strayed off, and challenged rivals to a fight, while the cows tossed their heads and kicked out with their hooves at too persistent suitors. Many times an 'army' of them passed by, covering us with dust. Once a herd of many hundred zebras galloped past our car, their thundering hooves stirring up a pall of dust; when they had almost passed by, through the cloud of dust I saw a lion leaping upon the last of the zebras; he missed his prey and so did a second lion who sprang a second later.

That evening when we returned to the ravine we found the cubs looking very tired. Jespah was particularly lethargic and rested near my car, and whenever Little Elsa came by he licked her and later joined her when she went a little distance away and embraced her. Gopa was already at the meat but it was only after Little Elsa plucked up courage and started on her supper that Jespah came for his cod-liver oil. After this he spent the night close to my car.

Next morning we decided to explore the forty-mile valley in which was the cubs' ravine. For a while we were able to follow a car track, then it faded out and we were obliged to plough our way through shoulder-high grass and whistling thorns. The farther we drove the more we were plagued by tsetse. In the circumstances, we naturally saw very little game; only rhino seemed to favour this spiky wilderness.

The valley ended in a wide open plain in which stood a solitary borassus palm, a species which usually grows near water; beside it was a herd of topi, which we estimated to number over three thousand head. We had never before seen so large a herd.

It had taken us five hours to cover thirty-five miles and we decided to make a detour of eighty-five miles rather than face the ordeal by tsetse, ants and thorns on our return journey, so we drove on to the great plain, where we met many vast herds of game, some of which were using giraffes as sentinels to warn them of the approach of lions, of which we saw several prides.

It was late afternoon when we got back to the cub valley and we were delighted to find the cubs waiting for us. We hoped it might be a sign that they were abandoning their purely nocturnal habits and learning to behave like the lions of the Serengeti, which, assured of their safety, spend their days in the open.

Next day we drove out to get a new 'kill'. On our return we found a letter from the director in which he confirmed in writing that we must leave the Serengeti on the 31st May and added that between now and then we were not permitted to bring any more meat into the camp to feed the cubs.

We drove up to the ravine and found the cubs waiting for us. Jespah was off his feed, did not touch any of the meat and seemed listless. We wondered whether, although it appeared healthy, the open wound round the arrowhead had become infected. Another possibility was that like Elsa at the time of her first release in country very similar to the Serengeti, he had developed an infection due to tsetse fly or ticks and was suffering from fever. He had been listless for a couple of days; now his condition was alarming.

Next morning, feeling anxious about him, we walked along the edge of the cubs' ravine and looked through our field-glasses to see if we could catch sight of him. In time we did see the cubs but they spotted us and, alarmed by our presence, rushed towards the cliff. I called to them but they went off.

Today the peace of the valley was disturbed by the ceaseless barking of large herds of zebra who rushed along as though compelled by some invisible power. The leaders sometimes stopped for a moment, perhaps to investigate the terrain, but soon made up for the pause by pushing ahead at increased speed. Our zebras were only a group which had broken off from the main body which numbered some twenty-five thousand head. On our way home we walked up the hill which separated the main valley from the cubs' ravine and from there we could see the mass of zebras, surrounded by about two hundred buffaloes looking like black islands in the striped sea. The whole column was moving quickly.

Next evening the cubs only appeared after dark. This was disappointing as it showed that they were not yet prepared to abandon their nocturnal habits.

After one lap of cod-liver oil Jespah retired behind the car; when the other cubs had eaten they went over to him and tried to make him play with them, but, though he licked them, he wouldn't move.

At dawn Gopa and Little Elsa had another meal and then went over to Jespah and tried to prod him into going to the ravine with them. After a time he rose slowly and began to follow them. I called and he returned and stood in front of me. I pointed to the meat and talked to him, as I did when I had wanted Elsa to eat,

61

and he reacted as his mother used to – went over to the 'kill' and began his meal. It was the first time in three days that we had seen him eat.

Having found I still had some terramycin I decided to start treating Jespah with it that evening for it was only too evident that he was ill. It was unthinkable that we should leave him in this state. Meanwhile we had no food to give him. So, as we were very short of time, George took it upon himself to drive forty miles outside the boundary of the park to shoot a 'kill'. We realised that this was contrary to our instructions but we hoped that in the circumstances we might be forgiven. Near the border we noticed a low-flying aircraft which was we imagined, carrying out a migration census. On our return to camp the park warden who had been a passenger in the plane and had seen George's 'kill' met us and asked us to explain why we had shot an animal in defiance of the prohibition. We apologised, told him of the circumstances and begged him to extend our permit to camp near the cubs. He said that he was not in a position to grant the extension and advised us to get an interview with the director at Arusha. This meant either a two hundred and fifty mile journey by road or chartering an aircraft. The warden kindly offered to hire a plane for me by radio from Nairobi. It was to collect me next morning. That night we spent as usual with the cubs. When I left at dawn, Jespah was still in the same listless state.

I had been invited to lunch with the director. He was displeased at George's shooting of the last 'kill' against his orders. I apologised and explained our predicament. He then suggested that if we were not happy about the situation, we might recapture the cubs and move them to one of two game reserves in Tanganyika where we would not be subject to the regulations of the national parks and could stay with the lions if they were ill. But I was not anxious to move the cubs a second time. After I had rejected this proposal the director agreed to extend our permit to enable us to stay eight more days with the cubs and to allow us to make three more 'kills' outside the Serengeti between now and the 8th June when we had to leave. He offered to arrange for a meeting between ourselves and the chairman of the trustees if we wanted to put our case before them and ask for more help than he himself could give us.

I arrived back at the camp in a heavy rainstorm feeling depressed. I went up at once to the ravine to join George but no cubs appeared that night and all we heard was the barking of zebra. We searched for the cubs in the morning but found no trace of them.

That evening the cubs arrived soon after dark. But later a faint lion call attracted their attention and they went off in the direction it came from. During their absence we were kept busy chasing hyenas away from the carcase; but they only left when the cubs returned. They quickly ate some more of the meat and then retired into the ravine. As soon as they had gone the hyenas came back and stayed till we hoisted the 'kill' out of their reach. On the following night the lion called again, and the cubs who had hardly touched their dinner went off in his direction. On the third evening Gopa and Little Elsa were very hungry and ate ravenously, but Jespah didn't eat. His condition, thanks no doubt to the terramycin, had improved but he was still far from well, so we decided to take advantage of the director's offer to put our problem to the chairman and beg for a further reprieve. Leaving George in charge of the cubs, I drove one hundred and twenty miles to his farm and had lunch with him.

He believed that the cubs should from now onwards be allowed to face the benefits and hazards of wild life. I suggested that while we were prepared to respect the policy of all national parks, which is to let nature take its course, I knew of many instances in which wardens of the East African Parks had helped ill or starving lions through a critical period, and pointed out that this was in fact an interference with the natural course of events. I stressed that Jespah had received his arrow wound because since early cubhood he had been deprived of a natural life and that we therefore felt responsible for helping to cure his injury.

I told the chairman how anxious we were that the release should be a complete success. This was unlikely to be the case if we abandoned the cubs before they were old enough to have become competent hunters. However, my arguments did not cause him to alter his point of view or change the date for our final departure.

63

On my way home I was obliged to camp the night and as I considered our problem it suddenly occurred to me that no one could prevent me from staying on in the Serengeti as a tourist provided I submitted to all park regulations. True, I would have to camp at one of the official sites near Seronera, which would mean a double journey of fifty miles daily to the ravine, I would not be allowed to be out at night and there would be no question of feeding the cubs. Still, I would be able to see how they were getting on and this seemed to be the best I could hope for.

It was already the 5th June, and as we had only three days left I thought it best to drive straight to Seronera and book a camping site. I was told that my request to stay as a tourist would need to be submitted to the director and would further require the approval of the chairman. Hoping for the best I put in my application and returned to camp.

Eager to make the most of the few days that remained, we drove to the ravine but the cubs didn't appear till the evening. When Jespah arrived he took his medicine, Gopa rushed at the meat and Little Elsa went off after some zebra which were barking in the distance. It always surprised me that, after dark, animals as vulnerable as zebra should invite trouble by announcing their presence to every predator in the neighbourhood by their barking, but they seemed to have no sense of prudence. This evening the noise went on until Jespah and Gopa joined their sister; then there was a thundering of hooves and the herd departed. Little Elsa came back very hungry and cuffed Jespah when he tried to share the meal, so he went away good-naturedly and sat a little way off till she had finished.

When we came to the ravine the next day and produced the 'kill' the cubs pounced on it. I hated to think that from now on they would have to go through a period of starvation before they had grown into competent hunters. At least Gopa and Little Elsa were in good condition but I felt very concerned about Jespah.

When it started to rain the cubs disappeared and George hoisted the 'kill', but they had not gone far. When they saw what was happening they rushed back to the meat and hung on to it till we feared the rope would break. When George lowered it they rushed

64

to it and seized the carcase by the throat, trying to suffocate the animal as though it had been a live beast. This was reassuring for it showed that they knew at least the first rule of killing.

On the 7th June I went to Seronera to find out whether I was to be allowed to join the ranks of the tourists. When I arrived I learned that so long as I behaved as an ordinary visitor I could stay on. I made my way back to camp with a much lighter heart, but was delayed by a pack of six wild dogs. I have never before seen a pack in the open and had not realised what handsome animals they are. Their name is rather misleading as not even a long-legged dog is so slender nor has any dog such big round ears; also wild dogs have only four toes, and are a separate genus. Their colour varies but is always made up of untidy patches of black, white and pale brown in patterns which differ with each individual dog, but each has a fine bushy tail usually with a pure white tip. Wild dogs are probably the most cruel and ruthless of predators; in the chase one dog replaces another till its victim collapses from exhaustion and is torn to pieces. Yet now as they lay in the shade of a tree scrutinising me I was tempted to rank them among the most attractive of wild animals. Obviously the dogs' bellies must have been full, for antelope grazed close to them without either showing any interest in the other.

When I came nearer to the camp I saw the dark-maned lion again; he was accompanied by his mate and another lioness who had two cubs; they looked about five weeks old. I felt sure that this was the pride which had chased our cubs from the release point some weeks ago. The lion allowed the cubs to crawl over him, but was much more interested in the activities of the other lioness who was stalking a small herd of zebra. Crouching close to the ground she advanced until she was within twenty yards of them, but the zebras seemed to feel that so long as they could see the lioness they were in control of the situation and showed no signs of alarm. Suddenly a Thomson's gazelle pranced forward daringly between the zebras and the lioness and paraded up and down apparently intent on teasing her. I expected to see the cheeky Tommy pay for his impertinence but nothing happened and when the zebras slowly moved off the Tommy followed them. Meanwhile the lion watched the proceedings, giving an occasional low grunt. Then he moved round an ant-hill to join his other mate and the two cubs. They played so charmingly together that I went back to camp to fetch George and we both returned to spend some hours watching them. Late in the afternoon heavy clouds announced a storm and we raced for home.

We had just time to park the cars near the ravine when a deluge broke upon us. It poured for many hours. The noise was so loud that it drowned our calls to the cubs and even when the rain stopped they failed to put in an appearance.

This was the last night which we would be allowed to spend in the open and, given the cubs' nocturnal habits, it might well be the last chance we should have of seeing them. It was therefore with great sadness that I heard the sleepy twitter of awakening birds and saw dawn break.

We searched for the cubs on our last morning; slowly we went along the ravine calling all the familiar names, but saw no sign of them. George had already started up the engine of his car when on top of the escarpment I noticed a yellow speck which I soon recognised as Jespah's head. I called and in response Gopa and Little Elsa showed up. We couldn't go away without saying good-bye to the cubs, so George switched off his engine and we climbed the escarpment.

Gopa and Little Elsa, unused to being followed into their fortress, bolted for the cover of the ravine, but Jespah sat calmly waiting for us and allowed us to take some photographs of him. Then he slowly went off to join the others, stopping several times to look back at us. Should we ever see the cubs again?

10 THE SERENGETI

It was after tea-time before we reached Seronera. George had to be over the border before dark, so he left in a hurry, taking Ibrahim, Makedde and the cook with him to Isiolo and leaving Nuru and the toto with me. When George had gone we began to pitch camp. We were improvising a shelter for our provisions when a cloud-burst soaked most of our possessions. During the night several hyenas prowled around and a lion came so close to my tent that I could hear his breathing.

Next morning we improved our camp. I had chosen a site on the top of a ridge within the area officially allotted for camping sites. Here, even if the rains were heavy we could be sure of not being bogged down and besides the view was superb.

Later in the day I went to Seronera to make arrangements for my stay and found that I had to hand in our fire-arms as it was against the regulations for visitors to keep them.

When I asked the warden what I should do if lions visited me during the night he grinned and replied: 'Shoo them off!'

Early next morning we went off with Nuru to look for the cubs; it was a twenty-five mile drive over skiddy roads to the ravine. We found the three of them lying under a large tree. It was nine o'clock by then and I had never before seen them in the open at such a late hour; I wondered whether they might have been awaiting our return. The cubs never tried to find us but had always waited for us to come and look for them. I thought that the cubs' present behaviour might show that they did not feel deserted and were sufficiently settled in their new environment to feel at home: in fact, that the release had been a success.

I called to the cubs, but they did not move, and when I got out of the car they bolted. I followed them in the car until Gopa and Jespah settled under a tree; by then Little Elsa had disappeared.

Next I went to the ravine to see what had happened to the last 'kill', but could find no trace of the meat.

I returned and seeing the two brothers still under their tree, I called to them, but they just sat watching me and didn't stir, so I settled down to write letters. Later Gopa went down to the river and after a while was followed by Jespah moving slowly. Two hours later a zebra thundered past, followed by a herd of impala racing as though in flight. Thinking that the cubs must be chasing them I drove to the place where I had seen Jespah disappear and nearly collided with a young blond-maned lion and farther down the valley I saw a full-grown lioness and later two others; but there was no sign of the cubs.

By this time it was necessary to start back for Seronera. We had trouble with the car and next morning by the time the garage had put it right it was 10 a.m., so I had little hope of finding the cubs in the open at the hour at which we would reach the ravine.

Among the animals we met the following morning were a herd of fifty head of impala. With their lyre-shaped horns, slender well-proportioned bodies and rich red colouring, they are among the most beautiful antelopes. At our approach one bounded away gracefully in long leaps, and soon the whole herd was jumping rhythmically. But that day too we drew a blank with the cubs.

The next morning we left early for the cub valley. The sun was still low and the plains were a sea of sparkling dew from which a mist arose. Wherever we looked we saw animals sleek or fluffy, striped, spotted or plain; with horns and bodies of infinite variety, all leaping and gambolling with a gaiety which was most infectious. We got to know a number of individuals quite well.

We spent some time observing the three lions which resembled ours so much that Nuru could not be persuaded that they were not Jespah, Gopa and Little Elsa. To prove to him that he was wrong I called to them but got no response and finally I put a dish of water near the car to test them. When he saw it the leader of the two male cubs growled at me and moved off. It was odd that three cubs about the same age as Elsa's should also have lost their mother, odd too that the lioness not only looked like Little Elsa but behaved much as she did, but neither of the male cubs had

68

an arrow wound like Jespah or a pot-belly like Gopa. After watching them for several hours I was pretty certain they were a strange pride.

Each day we started out full of hope and each evening returned defeated.

On our homeward journey the sun was behind us and we could watch the animals in a perfect light. The sunsets were superb, the hills turned indigo, the plain straw-coloured. It was dotted with dark brown ant-hills, on which cheetahs and topi often stood out against the sky, and now and then a lion's fluffy mane would rise above the grass as he lifted his head to prospect for his dinner among the grazing herds, while nearby ostriches fanned themselves with their wings and greater bustards strutted about pompously, showing off before the small guinea-fowl and francolins. The evening scene appeared very peaceful, yet I knew it was the pause before each predator set out to kill and fill his belly, and there were plenty of hyenas prowling about to remind one of the fact.

My nights in camp were often exciting. I could hear lions prowling round and got to recognise the voices of most of them. Once I awoke to hear lapping noises and, being half asleep, listened for some time before I realised that a lioness was inside my tent drinking out of my basin. I had nothing but a table between me and Africa so I shouted at her and urged her to go away which obligingly she did. On another occasion I was kept awake by the snorting of buffalo and in the light of my torch saw three huge beasts standing within twenty yards of my tent. Hyenas were, of course, always around. I often heard them clattering in the kitchen.

Although some of my nocturnal visitors made my heart beat fast, the roaring of the lions in the stillness of the night never seemed to me a 'blood-curdling noise', but a most wonderful sound and often appealingly gentle. The lions close to Seronera, having been used to visitors since cubhood, were particularly friendly. Many had been surrounded by cars while suckling their mothers and therefore had come to regard human beings and motors as a natural feature in their lives.

Except in areas in which people have hunted or shot from cars, the wild animals seemed to consider cars as some kind of fellow-creature with strange habits and a peculiar scent, but nevertheless harmless. Every day we met many lions – but there was never any trace of our cubs. We now searched as close as we could to the hills on the far side of the river. The dry season had come and the animals were now dependent on water holes and such rivers as did not dry up.

As the days passed in fruitless search, I became more and more depressed and finally wrote to George to come back and help me to find the cubs.

A few days later the director and a park warden visited my camp. I took the opportunity to renew my earlier request to be allowed to spend a few nights out in the car in the hope that the cubs would be attracted by the headlights and I also asked if I might be allowed to walk up the escarpment and in the hills, if necessary escorted by an armed African ranger. I stressed again the condition of Jespah's wound and the youth of the cubs. The director replied that at the trustees' next meeting he would put my requests before them; meanwhile he suggested that I should write to the chairman. This I did.

Soon after I was very thankful to receive a telegram from George saying that he would arrive on the 4th July. Meanwhile I drove and Nuru came with me to jack us out of the holes we got stuck in.

On my return from a day's search I found George in camp. He had been away nearly a month and had now taken ten days' leave and so anxious was he not to waste a moment of it that he had driven all through the night. In spite of a sleepless night George was ready to start off at once in search of the cubs, but first he gave me the director's reply to our appeal to the trustees asking permission to sleep out. It only said that the trustees had discussed our letter and that he was writing officially to let us know what they decided. Knowing that the park warden had been to Arusha and was expected back that evening I called on him hoping that he might have brought the letter. He had and this is what it said:

If we agreed to certain conditions they would be glad to grant our requests. George and I could sleep out for not more than seven nights and offer the cubs water and cod-liver oil if they came to us. During this time we were allowed to walk on the escarpment and elsewhere at our own risk and George was permitted to carry fire-arms for self-defence. We were to make no kill without first getting permission from the park warden and we were to keep the park warden advised about every other day of what was going on.

I asked the park warden: if we found the cubs emaciated while he happened to be on safari, how could we obtain permission to feed them? He advised me in this event to contact the director by radio and discuss the problem with him.

We then packed our cars for a week's absence. As a result of camping out among wild animals I have become a light sleeper and that night I woke to hear the distant engine of a car. Some moments later the park warden arrived and told us to move at once into the cars as a lion had taken a visitor from a camp near ours and was still prowling around. The man had been badly mauled. He told us that there was a charter plane in the area which could take the injured man at first light to Nairobi, then assuring us that there was nothing we could do to help, he left and not long afterwards we heard the plane take off.

Meanwhile George had told Nuru and the rest of our staff to light lamps and keep awake.

Very early we went to the scene of the incident, only three hundred yards from our camp, to find out whether the friends of the unfortunate man needed any help. Our spooring revealed that two lions had come past our camp and gone along the car track leading to the next camp and had stopped abreast of it. The spoor was that of two male lions; one was considerably larger than the other. The camping party had consisted of five people; three of them men who shared a tent. The night was warm so they had not put up their mosquito nets and had placed their low camp-beds in a row. They lay with their heads at the entrance of the tent which they left open. During the night the farmer in the middle bed, woken by a low moaning sound, noticed that his neighbour's bed was empty and disarranged. He switched on a torch and, fifteen yards away, saw a lion with his

71

friend's head in its mouth. He roused the camp, and two African servants very courageously rushed towards the lion; one flung a panga (a long knife) at it. Possibly this hit the lion for he dropped the man, bit viciously at the handle of the panga and moved a short distance away. The injured farmer was quickly rescued. Meanwhile the lion continued to circle the camp and was only kept off by having a car driven towards him.

Unfortunately the man's wounds proved fatal and he died on the operating table in Nairobi.

This was the first fatal accident to take place in the Serengeti since it became a national park. That morning two of the park wardens shot both lions. The larger one was found to have a septic wound in his shoulder, which no doubt was a serious handicap to his hunting activities. In such circumstances any lion in any part of Africa will not hesitate to kill a human being.

11 WE SEE THE CUBS AGAIN

The director arrived by plane that morning and we had a talk with him. He confirmed the concession to sleep out in the cub valley for seven nights but so far as preparing for feeding the cubs should we find them emaciated, he advised us not to cross our bridges before we came to them, and added that in an emergency the park warden might be able to help us. George had only eight days' leave left so we decided to make our preparations at once. However, before we could start we had to move our camp to Seronera, as in view of the accident no more camping was to be allowed till security measures had been taken.

As a result it was late in the day before we set off to the cub ravine. When we got there we parked our cars in the middle of the small plain where George had seen the cubs in May. No cubs showed up during that night.

Early in the morning we drove near to the cubs' ravine and climbed the escarpment above it where nearly a month ago we had seen the cubs. We walked along its crest for nearly three hours, calling repeatedly but in vain. Then we came down into the next valley and walked back to the car. As we reached the top of a rise which led into the cub ravine George grabbed me by the shoulder. There were all three cubs sitting by the cars waiting for us. They behaved in the most matter-of-fact manner as though we had never left them. Jespah came to greet us giving the soft moans with which Elsa always welcomed us. He allowed me to pat his head and then sat and watched us as we went over to the other cubs. They went off as we approached and settled under a tree. But when we offered them cod-liver oil and water they came and lapped it up quickly. They were thin but in fair condition though Jespah and Gopa had now completely lost their ruffs and looked like lionesses. Jespah's coat was no longer shining and he still carried the arrow. The wound was discharging a thin serum which attracted flies and which he licked repeatedly; he also had some small scars probably gained in combat with other animals. He was very friendly and came close to us but would not allow us to pull at the arrowhead.

It was wonderful to see the cubs again and as we watched them we discussed several puzzling questions. Why had the lions lost their ruffs? We knew that under stress domestic cats sometimes moult. Could Jespah and Gopa have become maneless owing to the strain of adapting themselves to a new environment? Why had they turned up today? Had they seen our car light during the night and realised that we were there? Or had they been hiding when I searched in the cub valley during the last month and been too frightened of my driver and Nuru to come into the open?

Though previously they had always taken cover during the hot hours of the day, now they stayed in the light shade of a tree while we lunched. When George went off to collect the second car which we had left in the plain, this didn't disturb them and for all the rest of that day they remained in the open. In fact they seemed to be adopting the habits of the Serengeti lions.

We had stored some of our kit beside our camp-beds inside the cars and the rest on the roof. Jespah inspected these objects hoping perhaps to find his dinner, and even Gopa and Little Elsa came close to us, but we had nothing for them but cod-liver oil. They settled close to our car and during the night we heard them playing. Jespah visited us several times, no doubt puzzled that we had not given him any meat.

After the weeks of anxiety it was a tremendous relief to know that the release had proved a success and that the cubs were in relatively good condition: the only worry was Jespah's discharging wound and his dull coat. But we did not want to take him out of the park separately if he could be operated on in the Serengeti. So we decided to use our week to try to get him in better condition and then try to make arrangements to have him operated upon. The days now at our disposal did not allow us time to do this.

Next morning we found the cubs under a bush about four hundred yards down the hill. Jespah came at once and placed himself between us and his brother and sister and I gave him his cod-liver oil. That morning his coat was much worse than it had been when we first saw him and he was covered with swellings the size of peas. This worried us but we did not wish to raise a false alarm about it until we were sure what the swellings were due to; they looked rather similar to swellings which Elsa had sometimes developed after rolling on ants. However, we could not be sure that this was what they were and would have to keep Jespah under observation. This meant feeding the cubs who would otherwise need to go off hunting.

George therefore drove off to Seronera to get permission to feed the cubs and to send a cable to the publishers of the Elsa books to give them our good news. In his enthusiasm he worded this telegram and also a similar one to the director at Arusha over-optimistically: 'cubs found in excellent condition'. This wording caused a false impression and later gave rise to a grave misunderstanding.

George returned without a kill; the park warden had been absent, so he had waited till the afternoon when he could speak to the director over the radio. He obtained permission to buy two goats at a small village outside the park, some sixty miles away, but since he could not get there and back in the day he had to put off getting the goats till the next day.

At dusk the cubs came looking for their dinner but as we had only cod-liver oil to give them they left early. Next morning George drove off to get the goats and I sorted out our kit and aired our bedding. The cubs arrived while everything was still laid out on the ground. This provided them with a splendid game, but they were very good-natured and in the end allowed me to collect all our possessions undamaged. After this they retired into the shade of a bush where they spent the rest of the day.

George arrived at 6 p.m. with the goats. The moment he saw the meat, Jespah seized it and raced away with it; Gopa and Little Elsa chased him and there was a scrimmage. The three cubs sat, noses together, holding on to the carcase, tempers grew hot and there were growls and spittings; for an hour the deadlock went on and not one of them would give way. Then Gopa made a try to go off with the meat, but Jespah grabbed it instantly and another

75

deadlock ensued. With ears flattened and giving angry snarls the brothers faced each other while Little Elsa quietly gnawed away. Finally they relaxed and the three cubs ate amicably together.

The second carcase we placed on the roof of the car, thinking it would be safe there till tomorrow, as the cubs had never tried to get on to the cars. But early in the morning I was woken by a heavy thud and found the car rocking violently. The next moment I saw Jespah jump with the carcase from the roof on to the bonnet and make off with it to the ravine followed by the other cubs.

A couple of hours later he reappeared and leapt on to the roof of the car where we had stored our surplus kit and found a lot of things there to delight him: cardboard boxes filled with bottles, my plant press, a rubber cushion, a folding armchair. Busily he emptied the boxes, clattering their contents on to the ground. When he had finished he rested his head on his paws and blinked at us. His brother and sister had watched him intently but had not ventured to join him; now they went off to play on a fallen tree where Jespah soon joined them. The three cubs prodded each other playfully for a while and then disappeared into the ravine.

We noticed a lot of vultures circling above the crest of the nearest hill and supposed they were leaving a kill, probably one made by the lion which I had heard roaring close by during the night. After lunch we went to look for the cubs and found them asleep in the dense cover at the base of the cliff. Next to them was the carcase of a freshly-killed reedbuck. Whether they had killed it or stolen it off a leopard we couldn't tell. That a kill should have taken place so close to us without our hearing a sound was odd enough.

In the evening we went back to the cubs and found that they had practically finished the reedbuck and had dragged what remains were left into cover. We could hear the lions breathing in the thicket but we could not see them. It seemed extraordinary that such large animals could hide themselves so completely – particularly as we knew to within a few feet where they were. Later the coughing of a leopard told us who had made the kill.

When it was dark the cubs came for a drink and spent the night near us but by morning they had gone off. After lunch they emerged from the ravine and Jespah hopped on to the roof of my car, while Gopa and Little Elsa lay under the shade of a tree some fifty yards away.

I sat close to Jespah and whenever my position allowed I tried to pull at the arrow. He made no objection to my twiddling the protruding shank, but it was as firmly fixed as ever and there was no sign of its sloughing out. The point of the arrow was just below the skin and a small slit might well suffice to pull it out point first. The swellings, probably due to ant bites, had disappeared, but his coat looked dull and shabby.

When night came we retired to our cars. Very soon the canvas roof of mine sagged under Jespah's weight and from my bed I was able to pat him through the canvas. Later George was woken by the swaying of his car and found Jespah leaning over the tailboard looking at him as though he wanted to come in. There was no sign of the others and Jespah himself left at dawn.

Tomorrow we should have to leave the cubs and we could have been fairly happy about them had it not been for Jespah's wound. However little it seemed to encumber him at the moment, it had obviously weakened his condition and was a source of infection as his dull coat proved. In combat with a prey the skin might get torn or the arrowhead packed deeper and either of these possibilities might cause serious damage which would ultimately impair his capacity to hunt. In the circumstances the sooner he could be operated on the better. We discussed the situation and decided to cut our time with the cubs short and leave as early as was possible the next morning, so that we could speak over the radio to the director and get permission to carry out the operation. For this we should need a crate in which to confine Jespah and a veterinary surgeon to give the anæsthetic and perform the operation. George was sure his leave would be extended for the time necessary to make the arrangements and get the operation performed.

We passed the evening watching the cubs licking each other and rolling about affectionately together behind the cars. They left about 11 p.m. This was the last we were to see of them though at the time we expected to return soon with a vet.

77

Later in the night we heard some lions calling in a low voice to each other and hoped it might be our cubs hunting.

Next morning we left for Seronera, hoping to arrange facilities to operate on Jespah at once. These were denied. We approached the director again. He advised us to appeal to the trustees who were holding their next meeting in August. With a heavy heart we left Tanganyika.

12 THE LONG SEARCH

When we got to Nairobi we wrote to the director of the Tanganyika National Parks, asking him to submit our request for permission to operate on Jespah, to the trustees at their mid-August meeting.

Towards the end of August we received a telegram from the director, informing us that the trustees had refused permission for the operation.

One of the most distinguished veterinary surgeons in Africa had already agreed to do the operation, should Jespah be found in a state which demanded an intervention. We talked to the Founder and Chairman of the East African Wild Life Society, and Major Grimwood about what we should now do.

We decided that Billy Collins, my publisher, who was then visiting East Africa, and I should go to the Serengeti and spend a week there trying to find the cubs. Billy would also see the chairman in Arusha and try to persuade him to change his mind, and allow Dr. Harthoorn, the veterinary surgeon, to operate, if this were possible and if he considered it necessary.

On our way through Arusha, Billy called on the director and discussed our wish to be allowed to sleep out in order to find the cubs and to have permission to operate on Jespah, if when we found him this seemed necessary. This conversation did not result in any change of attitude on the director's part; but they agreed that after our search for the cubs, Billy should see the chairman and talk the matter over with him. We then went on to the lodge at Seronera, where we spent six days.

Early in the morning after our arrival we set off for the cubs' release point. We found it occupied by a party of surveyors who had been living there for the last month. We asked them what lions they had seen. They had seen many, but could not, of course, know whether the cubs had been among them.

Then we went up to the cub ravine and I called Jespah, Gopa, Little Elsa, but there was no response. So we continued up the valley. Every time we saw trees covered with vulture, we drove up to them, hoping to find the cubs on a kill but were always disappointed. We found several pride of lion and at one point came very close to a herd of 200 buffalo.

Next day we went again at first light to the cub valley and searched along the river where, owing to the drought, there was a bigger concentration of animals than I had ever seen before. Finally we went back to the ravine and called for a long time but saw no sign of the cubs.

On our way home we saw a beautiful cheetah on his ant-hill and at a big pond a leopard and a saddlebill stork quenching their thirst.

By the fourth day Billy was obviously unwell. He had been unmercifully bitten by tsetse, his arms and legs were very swollen and I was thankful that a doctor happened to be staying at the lodge. He diagnosed an allergy, prescribed remedies and advised Billy not to go back to the tsetse-infected area. Therefore during the last three days of our visit we stayed close to Seronera. It was disappointing not to be able to go on searching for the cubs, but there was plenty of game to watch near the lodge, bat-eared foxes, lions, cheetah, and giraffe. We also witnessed the release of a rhino which had been brought to the park from an area where it interfered with a settlement scheme. It was the first release of this type and the chairman and his guests were coming to see it.

Billy took this occasion to give the chairman a letter asking him to allow the operation on Jespah to be performed.

The next day we again tried to persuade the chairman to agree to the operation on Jespah if this became possible and necessary. We did not succeed.

We soon heard that the meeting of the Trustees of the Serengeti had been put off till the end of October. This was worrying as the rains begin in November and though the park is not then closed conditions would be very bad for a search. All we could do was to wait till we heard the trustees' decision. Our proposal was turned down.

Now it was 30th October and we should have to race against the rains to get to the Serengeti and try to find the cubs before conditions made movement impossible. No one could prevent us from going on with our search provided we complied with the park regulations applicable to tourists.

Meanwhile Billy Collins had sent the director a cable expressing his concern at the situation and asking whether George and a Serengeti park warden might not be allowed to camp out in order to discover what condition Jespah was in. The reply received from the chairman gave the reasons on which the trustees' decision had been taken.

While all this was happening we were in the Serengeti under an overcast sky which threatened to release floods at any moment. We camped at our former site. The plains were teeming with large herds of wildebeeste and zebra and there were many foals and calves among them. In the ravine we found no trace of lion but when we drove on to the parkland valley, we saw a pride of five at a zebra kill and among them two young lions, one with a short blond mane and another with one equally short but darker. We remained there for four hours watching the pair until we were quite sure that they were not Jespah and Gopa.

We thought that one way of attracting our cubs might be by leaving our empty car out overnight by the ravine. The familiar sight might attract them and if it did so, next morning we would recognise their spoor; or they might even wait for us. We therefore placed my car where it could be seen from a long way off and then went home in George's.

On our arrival at the ravine the next day we found no lion spoor near the car and decided to leave the Land-Rover where it was for some time so we protected the wheels with thorns and removed the spare tyre, because hyenas are not averse to eating rubber.

When we got back to Seronera we found that we had missed the director who had been there during the afternoon. This was disappointing as four days earlier, on the 9th November, there had been a meeting at which our problems had been discussed.

By now the rains had set in properly and flooded the country. In spite of the difficult conditions, we crept up valleys, and into

81

the hinterland beyond the escarpment, but we never saw a sign of the cubs. We covered about one hundred miles a day.

Now it rained every day and nearly all day, and we were often bogged or had other misfortunes; once we burst two tyres while trying to cross a bad lugga and as we were changing them four buffalo watched us from much too close for my liking. On another occasion while we were working in pouring rain to fill in a muddy rut with brushwood and jack our car out foot by foot, two lions circled around us giving low whuffs.

We had a small compensation for our disappointment in not finding any trace of the cubs by being able to observe the reactions of various animals to the rains. One afternoon we saw a pack of hyenas hanging round some burrows which we had known for a long time but had never seen occupied. They must have had underground ramifications for now we observed animals disappear down one hole and then reappear from a burrow some hundred yards away. Among the hyena pack were a number of cubs who behaved like little jack-in-the-boxes, poking out their heads and then, when they saw us, popping back immediately.

A few miles farther along were twenty-two wild dogs, whose young seemed quite unafraid of us.

No one could remember such awful rains and it was estimated that 75 per cent of the animals had moved to the higher slopes of the Ngorongoro crater to escape from the swampy plains. We knew that lions were taking part in the exodus and wondered whether our cubs were among them.

The unprecedented floods often imprisoned us for days on end and camp life became very uncomfortable; the canvas got saturated and in my small tent everything was damp. We placed buckets by the tent poles to collect the rain as it ran off, in the hope of preventing the ground from turning into a bog. The buckets had to be emptied repeatedly and during the night they overflowed so that each morning I was obliged to wade through puddles which had formed on the ground-sheet.

When conditions allowed us to make another attempt to reach the ravine we found the plain deserted, except for a pair of ostriches with seventeen chicks who paraded across the marshy ground on their stiff legs, looking as though the place belonged to them; and indeed, there were only a few jackals to keep them company, four of whose cubs we found diving in and out of the holes of an abandoned ant-hill which they were using as a burrow. They were grey or side-striped jackals, a species we had never seen before. They came close to our car and were very inquisitive. Farther on we saw a pair of adult jackals on a Tommy kill; they left it when we approached and it was instantly covered by vultures. Then, like lightning, the jackals rushed back with flattened ears and scattered the birds. One dragged the meat off and began to tear at it as fast as he could before his mate returned.

We did not reach the ravine that time for we got bogged down and spent the rest of the day digging ourselves out.

When we returned to the lodge we learned that Prince Philip was due to visit the Serengeti on the 11th and 12th December and that during his time there no one except the staff would be permitted to remain in the park.

The weather continued to be appalling; there was very little game about and the lions near the lodge, which had been joined by another pride, had to go considerable distances to find prey; as a result, the cubs who were too young to accompany their mothers were often deserted for as long as forty-eight hours. When the lionesses as well as the cubs became emaciated the park warden sometimes shot a buck to prevent the mother from having to abandon her children while hunting. This helped the Seronera prides but I wondered how many new-born cubs far away from the lodge would survive these conditions.

It was a month since we had left my car in the ravine and when we reached it again we discovered that the rains had washed away all spoor so we could not tell whether the cubs had been to inspect it. Hoping for better luck we left it where it was. We drove ten miles down the valley but saw no game except buffalo. Tsetse were present in swarms and the canvas of the car was black with them.

On the 6th December two park wardens called to tell us that in connection with Prince Philip's visit we must leave Seronera from the 8th to the 13th and suggested that we should spend this time at Banagi, eleven miles away and on the border of the park. We asked whether we might not be given special permission to continue to look for the cubs during the days that the Duke was not spending in the park, but the director did not grant it. So we moved to Banagi.

After the 15th, we continued to go to the ravine, but never did we find a trace of the cubs. By this time George's car had to go to the workshop for much-needed repairs, so on Christmas Eve we got our lorry to take us to the cub ravine where my car was still stationed. When we reached it the driver went home in the truck and we drove on in my car.

It rained without stopping and we saw no sign of the cubs, so, towards evening, turned home very dispirited. When we came to the river we found that it had risen rapidly and was now 8 feet deep. This meant that we were cut off from Seronera and should have to spend the night out. It would be very uncomfortable but perhaps it might give us the chance we had waited for for so long, of attracting the cubs with our headlights. We parked in the open as far as we could from the river and left the lights switched on. They attracted millions of mosquitoes and other insects, and, as we had no Aerosol, we were completely at their mercy.

Twice we heard lions roar and hoped the cubs might come. But only a hyena appeared. She showed great interest in our rubber tyres and was not at all alarmed by our shouts, but bolted when she got our scent. I lay on the front seat remembering how we had spent the last two Christmases. Christmas Day 1959, when Elsa had suddenly reappeared for the first time after giving birth to her cubs and had swept our Christmas dinner off the table in her joy at seeing us again; and Christmas Eve 1960, when she and the cubs had watched me light the candles with so much interest and Jespah had gone off with my present for George, and I had opened the envelope which contained the deportation order.

Today bore no resemblance to those days and in the morning when I wished George a Happy Christmas, he looked surprised and asked: 'Is today Christmas Day?' All the same, I was glad I had spent last night in the car rather than in camp; but George felt that we should try to get back to Seronera at once, so as to prevent a rescue party from setting out to look for us and wasting petrol of which there was very little left.

We continued hunting for the cubs from dawn to dusk, and observed that the wild animals were gradually returning to the valley. Among them were three lionesses with five cubs. Thereafter we met them so often that they became quite accustomed to us and one afternoon when the lionesses went off to stalk a buffalo they left the cubs to 'stay put' so close to the car that we could easily have picked them up.

For a short time the weather improved, then the rain returned with renewed force. Our only chance of finding the cubs was to look for them on the higher levels. So, as far as the floods permitted, we decided to make a thorough search of the hilly area. To reach it we would drive across the plains, keeping where possible to the ridges.

We recognised that our chances of finding the cubs were not great, since in that vast area covered with rocks and woods, and broken up by cliffs and rivulets, one might easily pass within a few feet of a lion or any large animal without seeing him. Already we had several times nearly collided with a group of buffalo wallowing in a mud pool, concealed by the shoulder-high grass. On these occasions I held my breath wondering what the outcome would be, but the huge beasts proved as anxious as we were to avoid an encounter; they emerged as quickly as they could from the morass and cantered away tossing their great heads, only giving a few backward glances to see whether we were following them.

The ground was terribly soggy and as disagreeable to the animals as to ourselves; we had proof of this one morning when we saw a lioness and her two cubs high up in a tree obviously trying to keep dry. As we came up to take a photograph, the little ones fell to the ground, then the lioness jumped down but immediately led them up another tree. On this trip we also saw a very amusing sight: three jackals being chased by angry guinea-fowl. Whenever the jackals turned the cackling birds flew over the trio or pecked at them. At this the jackals rushed off with their tails between their legs to a safe vantage point from which a little later they made a counter-attack, but the fowl grew so aggressive that finally the jackals bolted.

During all these weeks the rains never ceased and our car gradually fell to pieces, as did our hopes of finding the cubs.

13 THE PRICE OF FREEDOM

We had now struggled for months against the worst possible weather, and under conditions which greatly reduced our chances of finding the cubs. So, when on the 2nd of February the director came to Seronera, I wrote to him repeating my plea to be allowed to sleep out since this was our best hope of seeing the cubs. He replied that it was not within his competence to give us such permission but that he would place my request before the trustees at their March meeting if I wished him to do so. By then Jespah, if he were still alive, would have carried the arrowhead for a year, unless it had sloughed out. Since, for the time being, we could do nothing more to obtain the permission we needed we continued our search, trying desperately to find a route by which we could reach the escarpment and its hinterland. We drove from dawn to dusk, over most difficult terrain, forcing the car up steep rocky slopes, jerking from boulder to boulder. But only when the rains had decreased did we eventually succeed in reaching the top of the escarpment and even in driving along it. The early morning and late afternoon were the most probable times for seeing the cubs but it was difficult for us to reach the area where they might be early enough, or to leave late enough because of the need to obey the park regulation.

When conditions became more normal some lions gradually followed the game back to the valley. Before the rains we had thought nothing of meeting twenty-five or thirty lions in a day; now if we saw nine we were greatly elated and our hopes of finding the cubs rose. We felt sure that we should recognise them not only because Jespah's and Gopa's manes would still be much shorter than those of other lions of the same age, but also because of their individual characteristics, which even if they had split up and joined another pride, would make them identifiable.

One evening the director again visited us and I suggested that

I might put our case before the trustees at their March meeting myself. The trustees agreed, so, when the time came, I started off for Arusha, leaving George to search for the cubs. As I drove across the plain I saw that great herds of wildebeeste and zebra were returning to it from the high ground. While it had been devoid of game we had not searched the area, but I thought that when I returned we must see whether our cubs might not be among these herds.

I asked the executive committee for permission to sleep out and if we did find the cubs to be allowed to decide afterwards what it would be best to do about Jespah. My request was turned down.

When I told George the outcome of the meeting he decided to appeal to the Minister of Lands, Forests and Wild Life of Tanganyika, and wrote to Minister Tewa asking for permission to sleep out and also to continue our search in the Serengeti during the rainy period. The reply was negative.

During the time that was left to us before the next rainy season in April and May we determined to concentrate our searches in the areas which were free of tsetse and should it prove necessary, we would return in June and continue to look for Jespah. When the park warden returned from a safari he told us that he had seen the lame young lion which a white hunter had also recently seen. He was still in company with another lion who was plainly providing him with food, since he could not hunt for himself. The park warden had shot two Tommies to help him out, but doubted if he would recover and said he meant to keep an eye on him and put him out of his misery if it seemed necessary. On hearing this, even though the warden had assured us that the lion could not be Jespah as he had no wound or scar, we set off at once to find the injured animal. On our way we met a safari party who told us that they had seen two very thin young lions one of which limped. We did not think this could be the warden's pair for they were ten miles away from where he had observed them and the lame animal could hardly have covered such a distance.

We drove on through thousands of Tommies, zebra, Grant's gazelle, and wildebeeste among which we saw a flock of over a hundred ostrich chicks led by a single cock. This was quite a wingful to be guarded only by one cock, and he seemed aware of his responsibility, for he charged away at top speed, giving us little time to take a picture.

One morning we saw a young blond lion and three lionesses on a kopje; they let us come close to them, and the lion, though he seemed older than Jespah, looked tantalisingly like him. I could only hope that one day he too would have his harem and be equally happy. When we saw the pride again late in the afternoon they were in the plain and evidently selecting a prey for their evening meal from among a group of three zebra and a foal which were grazing unsuspectingly about four hundred yards away.

One of the lionesses advanced, her belly close to the ground; after thirty yards she stopped to let the rest of the pride catch up with her; the lion brought up the rear. Then a different lioness took the lead and led the party forward another thirty yards. They were within seventy yards of their prey before one of the zebra noticed them. The lions, seeing they had been spotted, froze; the zebra looked calmly at them and continued feeding. Meanwhile the foal moved towards the pride as it grazed. Everything around was quiet and peaceful and it was distressing to see the little zebra so innocently approaching the lions; they seemed to be in no hurry and just sat in a line, watching. Well, the lions had to live and who was to criticise them for killing in order to survive.

When the light faded we had to drive home so we were spared seeing the end of the stalk, but perhaps the foal escaped, for next day when we came to the place expecting to find the pride on a kill, there was no carcase, nor were any lions to be seen. A few miles farther away, we found three lionesses devouring a freshly killed wildebeeste. One of them was carefully removing the hairs of the beard and spitting them out. She reminded me of Elsa, who always detested tickling hairs and feathers and although she loved guinea-fowl refused to eat one unless we had first plucked it for her.

Circling round Naabi Hill on our way back, we saw a pride of eight lion and stopped the car; immediately a young male rushed up and sat close looking at us. He was so strikingly like Jespah that we even wondered whether he might be our cub, but he showed no scar and his expression was different. All the same we wanted to test him, but could not wait to do so because of the need to be back at Seronera by nightfall.

Very early next morning we set out to look for him again. The pride had only moved a short distance into the plain; they were dozing and too replete to bother about us, except for the young lion who came up, circled the car and behaved in such a friendly manner that doubts again assailed us. Could he be Jespah? The pie-dish would be the conclusive test. We held it out: the cub looked at it with complete indifference. Then his brothers and sisters plucked up courage and came to play around the car. We had to resign ourselves to the fact that these were not Elsa's children, though the largest male cub had many characteristics in common with him, including the habit of keeping watch over the pride whilst the adults rested and recovered their energy for the night's hunting. Once this young lion had satisfied himself that we were harmless he went over to his father and snuggled up to him but, head on paws, continued to watch us through half closed eyes, long after the rest of the pride had gone to sleep.

By now we had almost given up hope of finding the injured lion, though we were anxious to do so, to make quite certain that he was not Jespah; one day, we found him by a rainpool. His companion was with him, and not far away were two young lions with short ruffs. The four seemed to have formed a bachelor party; we hoped it was for the purpose of helping the sick lion. At our approach he pulled himself up into a standing position, but carefully sat down again for obviously it hurt him to put weight on the injured leg. His rump was withered, he was very thin, and the expression of his eyes showed that he was in pain. A first glance had told us that he was not Jespah, but I was tormented by the idea that our cub might be in a similar state. We would have liked to have shot a buck for the invalid and had asked if we might do so should we find him in distress, but were told that we could not have permission to make a kill. We therefore left him hoping that his companions would provide for him.

We had not much time left before we should be forced to leave the Serengeti for two months, so as we knew that by now we had investigated the lion population round Naabi Hill pretty thoroughly, we decided to spend our last days examining the cub valley. The animals had by now returned to their normal habits and the area was well stocked with game.

During our final days in the park we drove non-stop from sunrise to dark hoping that we might still get a sight of the cubs before we had to leave. We had spent five months in the Serengeti, much of it under appalling weather conditions, we had driven ceaselessly, making demands on our bodies and on our vehicles that they were scarcely able to endure, we had searched every accessible place in which we thought the cubs might be. It had all been fruitless. The only positive results were that we had got to know the wild animals in the area and been able to study their behaviour during the rains and we left a network of car tracks that would be useful to the wardens in reaching hitherto inaccessible parts of the Serengeti.

On our last day we were guided by vultures to a buffalo kill near to the place where five days previously we had seen the two lions that looked so like an older Jespah and Gopa. To our surprise there they were, once more devouring a buffalo, though why they should choose to tackle these formidable beasts instead of the vulnerable kongoni and smaller antelopes we could not understand.

The dark lion who resembled Gopa, replete to bursting point, was guarding the kill against three cheeky jackals, who seized every opportunity to sneak a bite, till a growl sent them running off to avoid a cuffing. The blond lion took no part in the defence, but lay in the shade of a tree, his mane ruffled by the morning wind.

How splendid these lions were – aloof, but friendly, dignified and self-possessed. Looking at them it was easy to see why the lion has always fascinated man and become a symbol of something he admires. The king of animals, as they have called him, is a tolerant monarch; true, he is a predator, but predators are essential to keep the balance of wild life and the lion has no wish to harm, he does not attack man unless he is persecuted for his skin or when he is too infirm to find other more active prey. He never kills except to satisfy his hunger as is proved by the unconcern with which herds graze around a pride when they know that the lions' bellies are full.

How I loved watching this scene in front of me. I thought of Elsa's children. Where would they be at this moment? My heart was with them wherever they were. But it was also with these two lions here in front of us; and as I watched this beautiful pair, I realised how all the characteristics of our cubs were inherent in them. Indeed, in every lion I saw during our searches I recognised the intrinsic nature of Elsa, Jespah, Gopa and Little Elsa, the spirit of all the magnificent lions in Africa. May God protect them from any arrow and bless them all and their Kingdom.

Serengeti, June 1962

Born Free

The Story of Elsa

JOY ADAMSON

Elsa was born free, a lioness of Kenya, but when she was several weeks old, her mother was killed. So the Adamsons adopted her. Elsa slept on their beds, licked their faces with her sandpaper tongue, and knocked them to the ground with her paw as her own special joke! She chased elephants, stalked rhinos and played hide and seek with gazelles.

But the time came when she grew restless, and the Adamsons decided to return her to her natural life in the wild. Their attempts were hazardous and painful, for Elsa had to be accepted by her own kind, and more vital, she had to learn to kill for herself if she were to survive.

Joy Adamson's famous books about Elsa, *Born Free* and *Living Free* have inspired two of the most popular animal films of all time. *Living Free* is also an Armada Lion.

Living Free
Elsa and Her Cubs

JOY ADAMSON

At the end of *Born Free*, the Adamsons had re-introduced Elsa, the Kenya lioness to the wild. But when Elsa gave birth to three cubs, Jespah, Gopa and little Elsa, she had no pride to help her feed and protect them. So once more she returned to the Adamsons' camp.

In the camp the cubs played 'ambush', swept tables clean with the swipe of a paw, dragged off field glasses and guinea fowl, and chewed at the tents. For a year the Adamsons watched the cubs grow in strength and instinct. Then they left Elsa and her family, for the lions were creatures of the wild, living free.

Joy Adamson's famous books about Elsa, *Born Free* and *Living Free* have inspired two of the most popular animal films of all time. *Born Free* is also an Armada Lion.

Panther

RODERICK HAIG-BROWN

Ki-yu's father had been the meanest panther on Vancouver Island. Ki-yu grew up to be just as mean and even more cunning. Every living thing became his enemy – man especially.

The seasons passed in killing, feeding, and roaming, sometimes with a mate, sometimes alone. With his brute strength Ki-yu brought down deer, wolves, and even a bear. Then out of daring and disdain he came down from the mountains to attack the farm animals. And so he became the hunted as well as the hunter.

David Milton was the best panther hunter on the island. For two years he pursued Ki-yu relentlessly, tracking him with all his skill and knowledge, only to lose him time and again.

But both the panther and the man knew that in the end only one of them could survive. . .

King of the Wind

MARGUERITE HENRY

Sham was faster than the wind, for he bore the white spot on his heel, symbol of speed. But upon his chest was the wheat-ear, mark of ill-luck – these two signs were to rule his life.

He was born in the Royal Stables of Morocco and was prized for his beauty and speed. Then circumstance leads him to France and England where disaster follows cruel disaster. But his spirit cannot be broken. . .

And with him always is Agba, the Arab horse-boy who loves him.

Misty of Chincoteague, *Sea Star* and *Stormy* are more wonderful books about horses by Marguerite Henry available in Lions.